Supporting the Emotional Work
of School Leaders

✓

Other Books in the Series:
Durrant and Holden, *Teachers Leading Change* (2006)
Fink, *Leadership for Mortals* (2005)
Woods, *Democratic Leadership in Education* (2005)
Bottery, *The Challenges of Educational Leadership* (2004)

Supporting the Emotional Work of School Leaders

Belinda Harris

P·C·P
Paul Chapman
Publishing

Paul Chapman Publishing
SAGE Publications Ltd
1 Oliver's Yard
55 City Road
London EC1Y 1SP

SAGE Publications Inc.
2455 Teller Road
Thousand Oaks, California 91320

SAGE Publications India Pvt Ltd
B 1/I 1 Mohan Cooperative Industrial Area
Mathura Road
New Delhi 110 044

SAGE Publications Asia-Pacific Pte Ltd
33 Pekin Street #02-01
Far East Square
Singapore 048763

Library of Congress Control Number: 2007920095

A catalogue record for this book is available from the
British Library

ISBN 978-0-7619-4467-6
ISBN 978-0-7619-4468-3 (pbk)

Typeset by Dorwyn, Wells, Somerset
Printed in Great Britain by Athenaeum Press, Gateshead,
Tyne & Wear
Printed on paper from sustainable resources

For Callum and Jamie
with love

Contents

Acknowledgements

I am indebted to many people for their help and support with this book, especially the leaders, teachers and pupils who contributed to the research projects and the members of project steering groups.

I should also like to thank the following people for their emotional and practical support throughout the past months: my colleagues in the Centre for the Study of Human Relations for covering my teaching and administration; Patricia Thomson, Richard Reep and Maggie Maronitis for their care and supportive feedback on ideas and drafts at different stages; Jack, Callum and Jamie for their forbearance.

Special thanks are due to Alma Harris for her unstinting care, encouragement and belief in me. Her generosity of spirit made all the difference.

The author and publisher would like to thank Stephen Karpman for the use of Figure 3.1 on p. 39 Karpman's Drama Triangle.

Foreword

In politics 'it is much safer to be feared than loved' wrote Machi-avelli in *The Prince* in 1515. This is a premise that has been rein-forced in much of the subsequent writing about leadership and leadership development. Command and control approaches to leadership can be found today quite explicitly in the discourses around failing schools where a 'strong' head is often required to take charge and turn the school around. The only problem is that while control and fear often bring quick results the long term prognosis is less favourable. Schools in difficulty soon return to normative prac-tice when the 'strong head' leaves or when there is little left in the leadership repertoire to take the school to a different stage in its development. So while the rational, strategic and instrumental models of leadership remain compellingly attractive, they can only take us so far. The challenges of school improvement in the fast paced world of today cannot be resolved with sixteenth century approaches to leadership or models of leadership that simply do not reflect the contemporary educational landscape.

This book by Belinda Harris offers us an alternative way of under-standing leadership and leadership practice. Its central message is that leadership is fundamentally about emotional engagement and involvement. It argues that leaders need to be more attuned to their emotions and that leadership is fundamentally about the quality of relationships with oneself and others. It points to the need for leaders to be more actively cognisant of their own emotional histo-ries as these both shape and affect their actions and reactions. There is also a painful exploration of the damaging effects of leadership when it is misused, misjudged or misunderstood.

The strength of the book resides in the powerful interplay between theory, practice and personal reflection. Belinda Harris draws upon a wide range of theoretical perspectives from counselling, human relations and education to create an intricate theoretical framework for the book. She also brings a rich source of empirical evidence to illuminate, exemplify and reinforce the theoretical points made. The voices of teachers, students and leaders in this book illustrate boldly, clearly and in some cases painfully what happens if the emotional dimension of leadership is ignored or just profoundly inadequate. Listening to these voices it is impossible to discount the human side of leadership or to dismiss the important emotional work that all leaders have to do.

The author's main argument is that leaders can only be effective if they recognise, develop and actively acknowledge their own emotional well being. The emotional health of the school leader, she argues, is powerfully linked to the emotional health of teachers and young people. The book gives many powerful examples of the significant impact of appropriate attention and care upon individual self esteem and self worth. It also shows how emotional wounding and hurt, on the part of those leading, can be detrimental and damaging to those they work with.

In this book Belinda Harris addresses two main questions: what emotional resources do contemporary leaders need in order to thrive and how do leaders create the emotional conditions within the organisation to foster sustainable change? These questions are addressed skilfully, empirically and respectfully. But let's be clear, this is not yet another book about emotional intelligence or developing the emotionally intelligent school. In the view of the author and many other contemporary writers in the field the idea of emotional intelligence not only offers a rather restricted analysis of the emotional dimensions of leadership but also falls into the trap of offering sets of conditions, strategies and approaches for all leaders in all contexts. In contrast this book is very careful not to offer prescription, checklists or guides to becoming a more emotionally able leader. In fact the reverse is true. Through its careful crafting of theory, practice and data the book explores emotional awareness and care in all its complexity, never suggesting that the processes involved are either straightforward or easily learned. It allows leaders to connect with the ideas, evidence and activities in their own way, emphasising that emotional literacy is a personal journey.

In this book a range of concepts are explored including emotional awareness, self care, reflection and engagement. Leaders at all levels will be able to relate to the range of emotional challenges presented. Many of the chapters allow us to witness and engage with the emotional dilemmas and tensions faced in everyday school settings. They take us out of our comfort zone and make us reflect upon our own leadership practice. They hold up the mirror and show us that the real work of leaders in schools is primarily emotional labour.

This book is unlikely to generate indifference. There will be those who will react adversely to the idea that leadership needs to have any emotional component at all. There will be those who will not engage with the ideas because they are too threatened or too uncomfortable. There will be those who will see this work as long overdue and an important strand in the empirical work on leadership in schools, as I do. One thing is certain: we cannot rely on outdated models of leadership practice if we are to lead effectively in the schools of today. This book is a significant step forward in thinking about leadership practice. It provides an alternative lens on what leadership is and what leadership does. It does so with humanity, authenticity, understanding and respect for those who lead in our schools.

Alma Harris
Series Editor

1 Introduction

In recent decades the experience of students, teachers and leaders in schools has been directly affected by a range of external factors, which have fundamentally changed the character and nature of schooling. This book is premised on the understanding that whilst politicians claim success for education reforms by quoting improvements in numeracy and literacy targets they refuse to acknowledge or engage with the deeper-seated negative effects of relentless change on the psychological health of schools and communities. Neither do they confront the relationship between many of their educational policies and the crisis in confidence felt by leaders, teachers and pupils in many schools.

Many 'failing' schools for example, are trapped in a performance cul-de-sac with few means at their disposal for turning themselves around within the required one year period to prevent school closure (Harris et al., 2006). There has been relatively little consideration or systematic investigation into the emotional distress of pupils, parents and communities as a result of school failure and school closure,[1] but it is reasonable to speculate that in many communities this has contributed to a collective sense of hopelessness with associated feelings of being 'missed', let down and marginalised. It is my contention that the instrumental and accountability driven approach to system-wide reform has created more disturbing and challenging problems for society and schools to grapple with. This is a position finding widespread support in other countries (Elmore, 2003; Williams, 2001).

There is a real crisis in education best exemplified perhaps by the prevalence and seriousness of violence against teachers (NAS/UWT, 2004), by the numbers of teachers that have retired early with stress-related ill-health and the large number of newly qualified teachers that fail to take up appointments in schools or leave the profession within five years of completing their training (Carlyle and Woods, 2002). It is acknowledged that global capitalism, the rise of the technological society, the pace of change, the demise of traditional community support systems and the widening gulf between rich and poor have contributed to high levels of psychological damage in society. It is sad and possibly inevitable that the social and emotional effects of these changes are reflected back to us through the attitudes and behaviours of children and young people in our schools.

So, what does this book have to offer teachers and leaders committed to enhancing the educational experience of all members of their school community? In this book I draw on extensive personal and professional experience of working in schools, on empirical evidence and on the literature on teacher effectiveness, human relations, counselling, school improvement and educational leadership to propose a more dynamic, inclusive and relational stance towards school change. Unlike the task and performance models of school improvement that have dominated the educational landscape, the approach presented in this book places people, relationships and learning back in the driving seat of change.

Given this premise, there is no intention or pretence to offer a 'quick fix' to the current set of circumstances or to provide a set of techniques aimed at short term solutions. Instead, I am concerned to engage readers with the deeper personal, social and emotional challenges of change leadership, to highlight the intra-personal, interpersonal and inter-group dynamics that underpin and permeate school life. These dynamics may reflect healing, energising forces for good or the contaminating, emotionally draining forces of criticism, negativity and apathy. These aspects of organisational life are often noticed and felt at an intuitive level. They are less often acknowledged, understood and engaged with in ways that accept and affirm the underlying distress in schools and see it as symptomatic of something bigger which needs respectful, caring and firm attention.

It is my belief that despite working harder and longer hours to support children and to implement change, many teachers are pedalling against a policy current that appears so strong that teaching has become literally heartbreaking and soul destroying work. The research and experience underpinning this book have led me to the view that schools have all the ingredients to create enriching, loving communities of practice yet vital nutrients are not being harnessed to revitalise, enthuse and energise jaded professionals. The unique perspectives, passions and intelligences of young people, parents, teachers and support staff have leadership capabilities which, if honoured, embraced and nurtured, can lead to active engagement and participation in leadership practices and foster deep, sustainable, relation-rich learning and personal growth.

As a gestalt psychotherapist I bring a certain theoretical lens and set of values to the analysis of data. Three of these are worthy of mention at this point in my deliberations. I aim to provide the reader with some insights into the differently textured threads that are woven into the fabric of this work. Firstly, Kurt Lewin's (1951) 'field theory' is a point of view that I find useful as a way of perceiving events holistically. It is one map of the territory of human experience in relationship, wherever (for example, classrooms, playground, staffroom) and however (for example, pairs, groups, departments) those relationships are constituted. A field theory map of human experience extends the concept of holism, that is, viewing the person as a 'whole' intellectual, emotional, physical and spiritual being, to include the person in their environment, culture and community. This 'whole' way of seeing and thinking acknowledges and embraces the intimate inter-connectedness between the individual, the events that shape their lives and the settings in which these events take place.

In field theory the act of knowing is also a relationship between the perceiver and perceived as events are always perceived in relationship. Each individual is therefore an agent in the field as well as a recipient of others' engagements in the field and will construct their version of events in ways that suit how they position themselves and are also positioned within the field. There is, for example, an interactive field between myself the author and you the reader right now. As I sit here I wonder what energies, ideas and feelings you are bringing to my work as you read.

Secondly, this book is underpinned by a belief in the equivalence and equi-potentiality of reason and emotion in helping people to make sense of their lives and of their personal, social and professional identities (Parks, 2000). Schools are powerhouses of emotion as individuals engage with each other, with learning, with their values, and with the everyday pleasures, excitements and joy that occur when relationships and learning combine in creative exploration and discovery. They are also minefields of disappointment, envy, 'fear, anguish, depression, humiliation, grief and guilt', and not just for the teachers involved. In Jeffrey and Woods' (1996) study of teacher stress it is clear that children and young people also bear the brunt of teachers' negative emotions in the 'field' that is the classroom.

Most recently, worrying trends of violence have taken root in some schools as young people reflect back and act out the depersonalisation and rage they experience in their daily lives. Instrumental educational change has created a culture of mistrust, hostility and conflict (Halton, 1995) which studies of teacher emotions have largely avoided exploring in any detail.

Exercise

Which of the aforementioned emotional constructs most closely resemble your own experience of school and are there any that you particularly notice by virtue of their absence?

Finally, this work is premised on a humanistic view of human nature (Goldstein,1939; Allport, 1955; Maslow, 1970, 1971), namely that the majority of people have an innate natural tendency to engage with their environment in personally and socially constructive ways. In other words, everyone has agency and therefore the potential for different levels and forms of leadership, whether in relation to learning, administration, individual and collective well being or community relations. However, in the course of human development through childhood and into adulthood everyone experiences challenges to their core sense of self, self worth and self efficacy. Indeed it is the formative process of working through such experiences that supports maturation and enhances the capacity for effective relating with others, particularly those in authority. Unfortunately, many young people experience such intense and sustained challenges to and violations of their core sense of self that they are unable to engage with the process of maturation. Their interactions with significant others, usually people in authority, have involved the intentional or unintentional misuse or abuse of personal power.

In this way the political, economic and social conditions in wider society are heartlessly and aggressively acted out in both private and public spaces. Persistent experiences of being undermined, dismissed, shamed or traumatised by rage, for example, have a deleterious effect on the individual's view of themselves and act as inhibitors of personal growth, learning and agency. Furthermore, the earlier such abuse is experienced the sooner a habit of violence and aggression is internalised that is highly resistant to change (Rutter et al., 1998). In other words, being treated as an object, an 'It' rather than as a person, rubs off, especially when the social, political and cultural field reinforces this view of certain people as objects and when the majority view of 'normality' and 'acceptability' is used to oppress or disenfranchise certain minority groups.

A huge market in self help books perpetuates the myth that socially inflicted psychological wounds can be cured by individual's cognitive understanding and introspection. Deep, sustained healing, however, needs at least one sensitive, responsive and reparative relationship, which is experienced in a safe, consistent and emotionally containing environment. In such conditions the individual's pain and distress is heard, accepted and actively 'met' or responded to by gently challenging the internalised feelings of negative worth and value. Such relationships can be nurtured in school settings to support individuals and groups (Pattison and Harris, 2006; Harris, Vincent et al., 2006; Hudson, 2006). However, the relational stance that is promoted here transcends that of the traditional counsellor, pastoral teacher or leader. Whilst self awareness is accepted as the sine qua non of good citizenship and leadership, awareness and emotional competences are not considered to be sufficient. In fact, the competency model of emotional intelligence advocated by Goleman (1995) and others, may unwittingly collude with and reinforce an 'I–It' approach to relationships, whereby the right skill or phrase can be prized from the emotional toolkit to ensure that individuals collaborate in the implementation of personal rather than social agendas.

More creative relationships are needed, founded on deep inner awareness, knowledge and understanding of self in all constructive and destructive configurations. In this way, the self that engages with pupils, colleagues, parents, governors and the wider educational community is fully present (emotionally, intellectually, spiritually and morally), fully inclusive (in touch with the needs, wishes and preferences of self and simultaneously able to reach out and 'touch' the needs, wishes and preferences of the other) and willing to make a commitment to the co-creation of the field (to the spontaneity and creativity of the moment and the endless possibilities of what unfolds in the contact between both parties). Such relationships acknowledge our vulnerabilities and cultivate and refine our strengths together with the leadership capacity that lies untapped or is expressed through less socially constructive patterns of behaviour. Such relationships treat the other as a cherished 'Thou' rather than an 'It'.

To summarise, I argue that the current social, political and economic climate has depersonalised communities and cut people off from internal and external sources of care and support, making them an 'It'. It is the inability of governments to engage teachers' hearts and minds and to involve them as partners in policy making that is one of the key failures of school reforms and one which has had serious consequences for the power dynamics of relationships experienced in classrooms, staffrooms and playgrounds. The current preoccupation with and pressure to achieve targets leads to relationships characterised more by the exercise of power and control than by the co-creation of engaging learning opportunities and environments. The emotional work of leadership therefore involves facilitating and supporting each person's active engagement in meaning-ful dialogue, deep learning and collaborative agency. The unfolding 'co-created field' of the classroom, school, educational community or wider social environment is more likely to be experienced as a vibrant, life-enhancing space in which people may thrive and develop their own capacity for leadership. To be effective in this work the leader has a duty of care to attend to their emotional needs and recognise how these might otherwise undermine their most concerted efforts to support, care for and mobilise others. Once more I am wondering how you, the reader, are responding to this assertion on my part and how this interacts with your values and experience.

The empirical base

This work has been informed by my participation in a number of research and development projects. The data from these projects informs large sections of this book. My experience as a secondary teacher, curriculum and pastoral leader, community liaison teacher and school counsellor in deprived, yet vibrant inner city communities, has also contributed to my understanding of the emotional work of leader-ship and has informed my choice of postgraduate studies in human relations, counselling and psychotherapy.

In recent years hundreds of teachers on experiential taught masters programmes in Human Relations, Counselling, Special Needs and Edu-cational Leadership have developed my understanding and afforded me opportunities to visit schools and work with groups of teachers on spe-cific projects. There is a significant body of research evidence for the effectiveness of experiential learning in human relations for teachers' personal and professional lives (for example, Hall et al., 1988; Hall et al., 1996) and also of the transferability of this learning to school life in

England and beyond (for example, Harris and Biddulph, 2000; Harris, 2001). This personal and professional knowledge has informed a series of vignettes which frame specific chapters. The characters and schools represented therein reflect composite depictions of real people, places and events and highlight key issues or themes, without purporting to be based on rigorous research.

The primary data source for this book involved a project undertaken with nine schools located in a Midlands Education Action Zone (MEAZ). The MEAZ launched an Emotional Intelligence (EI) programme in February 2001 with the explicit aims of:

- supporting schools to develop an emotional intelligence strategy within their Strategic Plans and thereby create a facilitative climate in schools to develop and nurture the emotional intelligence of children and staff

- enabling children to be more effective learners and grow into more confident adults.

A number of strategies were put in place to facilitate the development of the EI programme, including:

- EI training and coaching for head teachers

- EI training for school staff

- training in relevant teaching and learning strategies and whole school approaches

- focused work with vulnerable children

- individual school projects to prevent exclusions.

A research project was designed to evaluate the effectiveness of the emotional intelligence programme. This formative evaluation was therefore supportive of the overall aims of the programme. It was deemed important to model emotionally intelligent research practices and involve a wide range of stakeholders in each school in a sustained, collective and collaborative inquiry. The emphasis was on encouraging the process of debate and questioning in order to reveal levels of consensus, conflict, contradiction and commonality to participants as well as the researcher. It was recognised that debate offers the opportunity for the generation and renewal of shared understandings and may therefore be valuable in fostering the conviction and consensus needed to implement new initiatives and enrich practices in each school. With collaboration at the heart of the methodological approach a protocol was developed to establish a base level of cooperation and trust between the researcher and different stakeholders in the school. The research process took place in three phases:

Phase One
Based on an appreciation of each school as a field an attempt was made to understand the culture and climate of each school within its specific context. An initial half-day visit to each school involved the following activities:

- An interview with the head teacher to establish their motivation for and hopes of engagement in the EI programme, their understanding of the school's climate and culture and of any particular factors affecting the school's capacity for success in the emotional domain.

- Interviews with other key staff who were unable to attend a staff meeting after school. These included kitchen staff, parent helpers and teaching assistants.

- A classroom based session with between 10 and 12 pupils to discover their feelings about school and their capacity for emotional expression and understanding. A circle time format was used with younger pupils and a small focus group format with older pupils (year 6 and above). At the end of the session pupils were invited to take photographs over a few days to record any events, places or people that sparked an emotional response in them. Different arrangements were made for looking after the disposable cameras during class time and overnight. The cameras were then forwarded to the researcher for developing.

- A meeting with the whole staff to introduce the purposes of and processes involved in the research. Staff engaged in a school culture exercise (Hargreaves, 1995) in which they reflected on stories of four types of school (hothouse, traditionalist, welfarist, survivalist) and mapped out their perceptions of their own school on a grid. The exercise was undertaken individually, discussed in pairs and then shared in groups. These groups presented areas of agreement and disagreement.

- Staff were asked to complete an open-ended questionnaire based loosely on a SWOT analysis in their own time and to hand these into the school office. The SWOTs were then posted to the researcher for analysis.

Phase Two
The researcher returned to each school for a further half day between four and six weeks after the initial visit. This time the activities involved:

● Further interviews with key individuals.

● A classroom based session with pupils in which they presented and talked about their photos. These were then grouped together to represent key issues. In some schools, pupils worked together to create visual representations of their collective emotional experiences in school. In others, individual pupils talked into a cassette recorder identifying their reasons for choosing particular images while the researcher worked with small groups to clarify positive and negative experiences.

● A focus group of staff from all levels of the school. In the infant, junior, primary and special schools all staff were present, apart from the head teacher. At the secondary school the group was comprised of a cross-section of colleagues with academic, pastoral and ancillary roles. Each group was asked the same core set of questions designed to interrogate the findings of the SWOT analysis in more depth. Pupils' photographic work was also incorporated into the discussions.

Phase Three
A third visit to the school involved a presentation of the research findings at a whole school staff meeting. At this meeting particular strengths of the school were highlighted alongside areas for consideration and development. A discussion of the findings gave space for misunderstandings or factual errors to be corrected. A revised report was then forwarded to each school for final comment.

Phase Four
A summary of key findings from schools across the zone and a set of propositions were presented to a panel of experts convened by the staff of the Education Action Zone in June 2003.

Data was collected from three infants, two junior, two primary, one secondary and one special school. In this book, the data will focus primarily on the findings from one school in each category, although all schools will feature at some point as supporting or contrasting data[2].

A number of other projects are also referred to in the course of this book and therefore a brief summary of each is in order here:

- Improving the Quality of Education for All – IQEA (Harris 2004)

- Schools Facing Extremely Challenging Circumstances – OCTET (Harris et al., 2006)

- Promoting Emotional Development – PED (CSHR 2003).

All of these research projects involved an integral focus on the emotional development of teachers. The PED project focused only on the emotional domain, whereas the OCTET project involved a consistent emotional strand to teacher and school development alongside other 'third wave' school improvement approaches (Harris and Crispeels, 2006). IQEA involved a limited focus on emotional development. In addition, some data will be taken from the Coalfields Alternatives to Exclusion (CATE) project (Harris et al. 2006), an evaluation of a Local Authorities strategy to eliminate exclusion. Whereas the research method and findings of three of these projects (IQEA, OCTET, CATE) are in the public domain, the evaluation of the PED project is still awaiting publication.

All data is presented in a format which identifies the type of school, the role identity of the respondent and the source of the data. These are presented as follows:

Type of school	Role identity	Data source
I = Infants	H = Head Teacher	SWOT = Paper-based
J = Junior	D = Deputy Head	SWOT analysis
P = Primary	Teacher	I = Individual
M = Middle	S = Member of Senior	Interview
S = Secondary	Management	FG = Focus Group
SS = Special School	Team	
PRU = Pupil Referral	TL = Teacher Leader	
Unit	J = Newly or recently	
	qualified teacher	
	CA = Classroom	
	Assistant	
	P = Pupils	

Therefore *P–H–I* represents an individual interview with the head teacher of a primary school.

Not surprisingly, all of the MEAZ schools had experienced difficulties and challenges in previous years. However, it is important to note that all nine schools had achieved higher than the median of their benchmark group in at least one subject, with primary schools showing a substantial improvement of 6.6% in 2001 (as against 1.2% nationally) in Key Stage One results and 5% (compared with 0.3% nationally) at Key Stage Two. Most schools had moved beyond reactive fire-fighting towards more proactive management approaches and several schools' School Improvement Projects had been singled out for praise by Ofsted and HMI. Whilst the MEAZ schools may not be a representative sample in terms of their location or catchment group, the sample is sufficiently large to draw inferences about the emotional work of leaders.

All interviews were recorded on tape and professionally transcribed and the analytical reports presented to each school were modified in the light of additional comment and information. The first level analysis was through comparative analysis of different narratives within the school context to develop a rich, thick description of emotional experiencing. The second level of analysis across the Zone schools, extended the comparative analysis to identify major themes and categories, and used grounded theory (Strauss and Corbin, 1990).

Overview of the chapters

The first two chapters in this book map the field conditions affecting the emotional life and experience of communities, schools and individuals and offer an overview of what is meant by the emotional work of leaders in this context. Chapter Two considers the impact of globalisation on the nature of schooling. As previously argued this context has had a negative impact on people's sense of their own efficacy, worth and well being. The phrase 'repetitive change injury' is intended to highlight the prevalence of traumatic stress in schools as evidenced by teacher and leader stress and the disturbing rise in mental health problems in young people. Schools cannot afford to ignore this phenomenon if they are to develop professional communities of practice in which leadership, learning and well being occupy people's energies and underpin their relationships. Chapter Three builds on the theme of relationships to explore the emotional conditions that support the development of inclusive learning communities. Developing emotional fitness, literacy, maintenance and depth is understood to contribute to sustainable personal and professional growth and school change.

Chapters Four to Nine draw on the empirical data to identify key factors that support the emotional work of school leaders and offer ways of nurturing these in self and others. Chapter Four focuses specifically on enhancing emotional awareness to help leaders remain in touch with their inner experience and to respond appropriately and authentically to the daily opportunities and challenges of leadership. Chapter Five identifies ways in which life experience can inhibit the capacity for emotional experiencing and relating to others. Developing awareness of these personal processes alerts the leader to the creative adjustments they made to the field conditions of their original family and community and enables them to be more accepting and empathic towards themselves. Such self-acceptance also embraces the less palatable, or shadow aspects of self. If kept out of awareness and unchecked these are likely to leak out and contaminate relationships with others, undermine trust and damage school climate. Equally, leaders are vulnerable to the effects of others' shadows and may need to protect themselves. Navigating a path through such two-way wounding is the subject of Chapter Six. This is followed by an exploration of the role of values in creating and sustaining inclusive schools. It is argued that stakeholders must be actively engaged in meaningful dialogue and supported to reach informed decisions based on common ground expectations. This requires rigorous attention to interpersonal and inter-group processes as schools seek to respond constructively to daily changes in the field conditions without alienating or disenfranchising those they serve.

If leaders are to create vibrant communities of practice in their schools and classrooms they must acknowledge that this is emotionally draining work. Chapter Eight therefore is concerned with developing cultures of care in which the leader's own needs and the needs of their colleagues and pupils are respected and attended to. This is not just a matter of work–life balance but of ensuring that time spent in school has enough joy, stimulation and opportunities for meaningful engagement in learning that community members feel energised and enthused by events and committed to each other's humanity and well being. Whilst evidence is offered to support this, it is recognised that this is an ideal scenario for many schools which find their efforts dismissed or sabotaged by a critical mass of young people and/or their families. It is easy for such schools to fall into despondency and develop a collective sense of hopelessness. An understanding of post-traumatic stress in young people and the repetitive change injury suffered by teachers and schools is offered in Chapter Nine. It is argued that new kinds of commitments and relationships are needed to create enough safety, trust and persistence for collaborative, cooperative, mutually rewarding and growthful learning.

Endnotes

1 Hargreaves' (2004) article on 'disgust' is a notable exception.
2 All data has been anonymised therefore the names of individuals and schools are fictitious.

2 *Leading in an emotionally challenging context*

Introduction

Let me take you to a school, an ordinary school in extraordinary circumstances. This secondary school is located in a large, sprawling urban context with high levels of deprivation. Unemployment levels are high, young people are disaffected and there is gun crime and violence. There have been several advertisements for a replacement head but applications have simply not appeared. Why? Possibly the challenge is too great for any individual or maybe this is not a setting that would attract many aspiring leaders. It could also be that the type of leadership required at this school and its community is in very short supply. This is not to say that the school requires an extra strong or 'super leader' but rather that it requires leadership that focuses on the emotional well being of the school as a priority. It requires an emotionally attuned leader to create conditions of emotional safety, inclusiveness and care in which staff feel valued and supported to be creative and brave in their learning and teaching, and in which young people feel it is acceptable to learn.

This type of leadership will be explored later in the book but let's return to the school. This school did not choose to be in crisis or actively seek to be under-performing. So what has happened? The answer, partly, lies in deep economic, technological and societal changes that have re-shaped and redefined education over several decades. There are some important fault lines in the education system serving to shake up the system in a radical way. However such influences are far from new.

In January 1643 shortly after the English Civil War had begun, Jeremiah Whittaker, a Protestant preacher, warned members of the English House of Commons:

These days are days of shaking, days of trouble, and this shaking is universal: the Palatinate, Bohemia, Germany, Catalonia, Portugal, Ireland, England. ... Though all nations be not shaken at one time, yet no nation so stable but it shall have a time of shaking.[1]

Whatever the causes of that period of widespread turmoil in the 17th Century, today the words ring just as true. Political upheavals, war, natural disasters, the rapidity of change – all contribute to this sense of being globally shaken. In such times, schools find themselves confronted with the emotional and behavioural fallout of economic and social upheaval on the psychological health of the community. It is important, therefore to be aware of the global and national trends that affect the nature of education and the lives of leaders, teachers and young people.

The rise in global economic trade has spawned multi-national organisations spanning continents together with the infrastructures needed to create and sustain global supply and demand. New technologies have been developed and designed to optimise efficiency and facilitate communication across countries. The language of statistics, efficiency, performance targets and managerialism are the modus operandi of this global capitalism. The economic context has shaped political agendas to articulate this new language and meet the needs of global business, economic development and international trade. All this shaking is seriously endangering the planet's ecosystem and is currently affecting the conditions within which individuals, families and communities live and work and the networks of social support and care that have traditionally sustained them. We cannot fully grasp the extent to which people's lives are being irreversibly affected by forces beyond their direct control. Sennett (1998) coined the term 'corrosion of character' to describe the destructive effects of political and social change on people's work lives. He refers particularly to the erosion of integrity, trust and sustained purpose in individuals. However, he posits that the solution to these personal confusions lies as much with community as with the individual.

Stark statistics on economic migration, political asylum, mental health, addiction, suicide and global violence are indicative of the widening gap between rich and poor and of the misery, oppression and despair of people caught up in the social, economic, ethnic and environmental fallout of global business. Ordinary lives disrupted by (extra) ordinary events leave individuals and families adrift, suffering multiple losses, ruptured relationships and a pervasive sense of hopelessness. What does all this turbulence mean for the future of education? Many schools already find themselves in the front line when it comes to supporting children and young people who are traumatised by direct experience of war, inter-ethnic conflict, poverty, domestic violence, parental mental health problems and abuse to name but a few. This book asserts that education and leadership have a moral and ethical role to play in helping individuals to recover from the psychological effects of these issues. School communities need to consider for example, how they can provide a buffer zone between young people and the outside world, a safe space where individuals can develop a sense of self responsibility, connectedness and trust in others and the ability to live well and purposively. Such process goals are not just compatible with academic goals but also essential means by which to achieve them. In this way the processes involved in engaging with social and emotional fallout can produce significant social, educational and cultural benefits for all members of the school community, particularly those in leadership positions.

Leadership

In recent years schools have experienced their own share of direct 'shaking'. Across the world widespread reforms designed to make education systems fit for purpose in an increasingly virtual, global context have produced powerful mechanisms of accountability and scrutiny. Central to this process has been widespread recognition of the pivotal relationship between school leadership and school effectiveness (Bennett et al., 2003). Although the theory and practice of leadership has been widely researched and debated in the business sector for more than half a century, it was only the decision to give schools responsibility for managing their budgets in England that prompted consideration of how to prepare and support head teachers for their role (Day et al., 2000). The resulting school leadership industry is supported by a burgeoning academic and professional literature in the field and a proliferation of postgraduate taught courses in educational management and leadership in higher education institutions.

In England the Labour Government set up a National College for School Leadership and a National Qualification for Professional Headship (TTA, 1997) therefore making not only a huge financial investment in leadership research and development but also centrally defining and regulating the substance and style of leadership development. England is not alone here and governments across the globe, from New Zealand, Australia and Hong Kong to the United States and Chile are all focused on the school reform agenda driven by accountability.

In this policy context many areas of professional jurisdiction and control of the school curriculum have been slowly eroded. The introduction of a National Curriculum and, more recently, centrally prescribed teaching strategies for literacy and numeracy in England have made traditional notions of school leadership appear somewhat outdated. Furthermore, workforce reform originally introduced in the government's White Paper *Excellence and Enjoyment* (DfES, 2003a) and formalised through the 'Workload Agreement' (DfES 2003b) has increased concerns about the further erosion of teacher professionalism and the implications for teacher training and school leadership (Wilkinson, 2005).

At the school level the White Paper has led to tensions between primary teachers, eager for release from classroom duties to plan their lessons and restore some semblance of work–life balance, and head teachers whose concerns about funding the proposed changes from their existing school budget is causing them additional stress (Easen, 2006). In secondary schools, workforce remodelling has led to many experienced teachers losing positions of responsibility and pay in newly streamlined organisational structures. As with all other 'shakings', whether natural or man-made, there are inevitably survivors, casualties, winners and losers.

Despite the political investment in leadership, there is currently a crisis in the recruitment and retention of head teachers in England. A recent survey of Local Authorities undertaken on behalf of the National Association of Head Teachers, for example, estimates that 28% of primary and 20% of secondary schools advertising for head teachers were able to find a suitable candidate (Howson, 2006). Moreover, the General Teaching Council for England Survey of Teachers (Hutchings et al., 2006) indicates that only 4% of teachers anticipate becoming head teachers in the next five years. This state of affairs is therefore indicative of a longer term deeper crisis in school leadership. Head teachers cite excessive workloads for high levels of stress. Recently published figures indicate a significant increase in reported head teacher stress (Daniels and French, 2006). This inevitably raises concerns not only about the mental health and well being of school leaders but also the longer term sustainability of leadership practice as the preserve, responsibility and domain of a single human being supported by a senior leadership team.

Similarly, the 'shaking' of schools has had a deleterious effect on the recruitment and retention of teachers (NAS/UWT 2004). A growing body of research connects rises in teacher stress to the ongoing restructuring of education systems (Dinham and Scott, 1996; Fullan, 1997; Carlyle and Woods, 2002). DfES statistics (2005) report 55% of all teachers taking sickness absence and 2,797,300 days lost through illness during 2004. Teachers interviewed for this book describe an involuntary feeling of dread when asked to do something, even when invited to participate in or represent the school at some community or local authority function or teacher development event. Teachers and leaders considered to be 'outstanding' by Ofsted report feeling exhausted and overwhelmed by their workload and therefore find themselves constantly weighing up how much longer they can maintain the quality of their work and also sustain the pace of change. Recent concessions in the accountability system acknowledge and relieve some of the pressure by giving schools responsibility for self evaluation. However, they also increase pressure by giving head teachers yet another burden of paperwork. In addition, a 'spot-check' system means that the threat of inspection casts a menacing shadow over the life and planning of a school.

Where schools do manage to meet government targets for achievement, school improvement research and theory highlights significant problems in terms of sustainability at the level of school change. Several studies (for example, Gray et al., 1999; Joyce et al., 2002; Fullan, 2006) point to the difficulties in maintaining change processes beyond the short term. The National Literacy Strategy in the UK, for example, increased literacy levels in eleven year olds from 62% to 75% over a four year period before schools entered a 'plateau phase' and were unable to progress any further. Sustainability therefore poses a significant challenge to those leaders who are committed to continuous school improvement to meet the evolving and ever-changing demands of global capitalism. It may be useful at this point to briefly explore what we know about effective school improvement at the present time.

Improving schools

The literature on school effectiveness and school improvement reflects the changing landscape of leadership through three waves of school improvement (Harris and Crispeels, 2006). These three phases move from a 'one size fits all' focus on 'ownership' of organisational change (when schools were struggling to adjust to new powers and accountability structures) towards organisational change coupled with classroom level change (for example, developing models of teaching and classroom observation protocols) and, more latterly, tailor-made school development with a focus on building capacity, developing collaborative school cultures, improving teaching, learning, enquiry and pupil outcomes. This third wave has supported individual schools, families of schools and school clusters through challenging periods of change with some promising indicators of enhanced effectiveness (Harris et al., 2006; Lodge, 2005; Harris, 2004).

It is this 'third' wave of school improvement that offers most to the development of emotional literacy in schools. For example, the author has been involved in two third wave school improvement projects, namely, Improving the Quality of Education for All (IQEA) and the DfES funded OCTET project, both of which are based on third wave practices and philosophies of school improvement (Hopkins and Reynolds, 2001). Both projects utilise group processes to generate change and improvement. At each school, for example, a school improvement group is selected to be involved in training and networking with other IQEA/OCTET schools. The main aim of this group is to create the urgency, energy and agency for change through developing, extending and deepening their understanding of instruction and the process of action enquiry and reflection. Both projects introduced an emotional component into the 'mix' of interventions (Harris, 2004; Harris et al., 2006; Reynolds et al., 2006). The teachers directly involved in these projects found this component particularly helpful in thinking through how to creatively mobilise and engage colleagues and pupils in change efforts. In one OCTET school for example, an explicit focus on the emotional climate in school was dismissed by an Ofsted inspector as irrelevant. Heartened by feedback from colleagues and students however, the School Improvement Group (SIG) and senior management were undeterred and chose to sustain their focus on the emotional domain alongside other initiatives.

There is no intention or desire to make spurious links between the focus on emotions and pupil outcomes and certainly no hard evidence of a direct correlation. However, within the total mix of the OCTET school improvement project the emotional domain is likely to have played its own part in helping the schools to improve their examination results (Harris et al., 2006). Feedback from teachers involved in the OCTET project suggested that an emotional perspective on school life had helped them to develop more sensitive, compassionate and fun ways of mobilising fellow colleagues and pupils in the linked processes of change and learning as well as helping them to understand the ways in which emotions can serve to inhibit and sabotage school development.

Research undertaken by the Tavistock Clinic in London over many years demonstrates that unacknowledged emotions exert a powerful influence on and between individuals in group settings. These emotional dynamics affect school climate (perceptions of events in school) and school culture (shared ways of being, understanding and behaving) for better or worse. Concerns about the sustainability of school change highlight the importance of engaging with the emotional undertow of the staffroom and classroom in order to nurture emotional awareness and congruence and support more open and honest dialogue about interpersonal and inter-group (departmental/team) relationships. Such emotional and intellectual integrity helps to sustain the momentum of change through the inevitable ups and downs of school life that otherwise sap the energy and commitment of staff and contribute to the 'plateau' effect.

Exercise

Reflect on your experience of the process of school change. What would you identify as the key facilitating factors that enabled change processes to develop well and to achieve their objectives? Equally, what would you identify as key retarding factors that have negatively impacted the process of change and contributed to their failure or partial success? Separate these out into technical, task-centred factors (for example, time, cover) and people-centred factors (for example, involvement).

	Task-centred	People-centred
Facilitating factors		
Retarding factors		

What is the balance between these two sets of factors?

If you had to prioritise three, what would they be?

What does that tell you about yourself?

What is most important to you – task or relationship?

The unexpected consequences of change

A key characteristic of the government's 'shaking' of schools has been a perceived lack of care for the views and experience of school leaders, teachers and pupils. Successive government legislation has been based on the counter-intuitive assumption that those who know and work in the system are the least well equipped to solve the problems within it. Little consideration has been given to the psychological impact on leaders and teachers of implementing an endless stream of contradictory and sometimes competing policies. Teachers are expected to implement change unquestioningly whilst also being creative and innovative in their classroom practice.

Schools are expected to raise achievement by teaching a centrally prescribed curriculum whilst maintaining an inclusive ethos in which every child matters. The command and control model of effecting change adopted by the UK government is premised on a critical parent/naughty child discourse or dynamic. Martin Buber (1937) a Jewish philosopher, distinguished between 'I–It' and 'I–Thou' modes of relating. In the 'I–It' dynamic the other person(s) is experienced as a thing, an object-like entity which can be systematised, analysed and broken down into its universal parts. In this way school leaders and teachers are viewed and treated as recalcitrant children who cannot be trusted to behave properly and who therefore need to be told in detail not only what to deliver but also how to deliver it. Their efforts are closely monitored and judged by the government's inspectorate. If they are perceived to fail, as measured by examination results, then they are publicly named and shamed via the league tables and financially punished for their perceived inefficiency and ineffectiveness.

The acceptable face of the autonomy espoused in government policies is therefore constrained and conditional on playing by the rules within fixed parameters and structural conditions. Furthermore, standardised criteria for determining success and failure take no account of the school's field conditions. In the poorest neighbourhoods the experience of inspection can leave teachers feeling as marginalised, disempowered and hopeless as their students (Lupton, 2005). In a similar vein parents of disaffected young people are financially punished and often publicly shamed for their perceived inefficiency if their children fail to meet set targets for school attendance.

Parents, schools and those who work in them are thus divested of their human qualities and treated as if they were a collective 'It'. The worth of a leader and teacher is judged primarily upon their ability to meet targets, thereby reducing the role to that of foreman on the production line. As we shall see later, this 'I–It' dynamic is a prevalent and pervasive by-product of shaking, serves to maintain hierarchical power relations and significantly contributes to many of the social problems that plague contemporary society.

The policy climate has produced 'frightened organisations', 'frightened parents' and 'frightened teachers' who manage their anxiety by teaching to the test to maximise students' results and minimise the threat of humiliation and punishment (Watkins, 1999). The language of education has become mechanised and much teaching is 'delivered' through teacher talk combined with behaviour management techniques. Students are required to digest passively the diet of facts and figures in a one way process of knowledge transfer. In this way teachers replicate the 'I–It' dynamic in their relations with students treating them as machines that have to be filled with the right octane fuel to ensure they are equipped to pass their road test. Apart from disempowering and deskilling learners this approach creates high dependency on the teacher and contributes significantly to the overload that stresses many teachers.

Muijs and Reynolds (2001) further suggest that whilst being a good technician is necessary, it is not sufficient in today's classrooms. Many students suffer, for example, the effects of loss, trauma, neglect and abuse. Teaching to the test does little to distract them from or soothe their underlying emotional distress and they are unable to engage in the process of learning. It is in the absence of an emotionally containing relationship that many young people find their levels of anxiety intolerable and act out their distress within the classroom, playground and school toilets. In some cases being treated as an 'It' merely replicates other negative experiences of relating with adults outside the school setting and triggers emotional responses that are out of proportion to the teacher's actual behaviour. Teachers and leaders in their turn may find themselves verbally and physically attacked and emotionally battered by the continual struggle to manage behaviour and survive some challenging classrooms.

In this cycle of negativity some damaged young people are labelled 'disaffected', shamed and punished therefore mirroring and perpetuating the government's attitude towards schools deemed to be poor or 'naughty'. In these ways the 'I–It' dynamic in the field conditions spawns more 'I–It' behaviours and responses. Capra (2003) distinguishes between life-enhancing and life-destroying organisations. The shaking of society and education has pulled many schools towards the latter end of the spectrum.

School leaders and teachers report being ill prepared for the emotional dimensions of their role (CSHR, 2003). They talk of groping in the dark, looking for quick fixes to reduce the incidence of challenging behaviour so that they can focus on teaching and thereby lift their own morale as well as that of colleagues, students and parents alike. It is not surprising that teachers cannot make the emotional connections necessary to break the cycle of negative relationships with students (and some parents) when their own experience is one of emotional abandonment and of relationships that disrespect and devalue their worth within school and society.

Research into school violence suggests that many schools unwittingly promote pro-violent behaviour through a lack of understanding of the developmental needs of children whose brain structure and functioning has been impaired by traumatic emotional experiences (Hoskin and Walsh, 2005). Martin Teicher's (2000) research into the brains of young children, for example, demonstrates that repeated exposure to stressful events hardwires the brain and bodily response system for over-responsiveness to even minor stressors and damages the corpus calloseum, which is the main highway for communication between the left and right hemispheres of the brain. It is not necessary to frighten a young child very much to establish a fearful response to the environment. Indeed being shouted at regularly and over time, a characteristic of many classrooms and corridors, leaves a legacy in the emotional structure of the developing brain that many teachers would not wish to compound in the way they do if they were more aware of the impact of their own behaviour.

Part of the task of leadership therefore is to alter the field conditions and move the school towards more life-enhancing patterns of communication and behaviour. A plethora of writers in education have highlighted the necessity for new forms of relationship to support organisational change and student learning (Hargreaves, 1998; Fullan, 2006; Fielding, 2006). Leaders and teachers have to challenge and transcend the instrumental and potentially damaging 'I–It' ways of engaging and replace them with more **attentive, attuned, accepting, affirming and appreciative relationships**. These five 'A's are the basic building blocks on which more healing and constructive relationships can unfold and evolve. As we shall see later, it is these relational qualities that speak to and soothe an individual's trauma and underlying distress. They are also a valuable antidote to the internalised shame that develops through oppressive relationships that attack an individual's core sense of worth and right to exist.

Improving achievement is undoubtedly an important goal of schooling. However, it is also important to acknowledge that for many young people and schools the preoccupation with examination results has exacerbated their difficulties rather than resolving them. The rise in numbers of temporary and permanent exclusions, particularly amongst already marginalised groups (DfES, 2006), the high turnover of teachers (Carlyle and Woods, 2003), and the escalation of violence against teachers and fellow pupils (Lambourn, 2006) are but the tip of an iceberg, reflecting not only the impact of 'shaking schools' on the mental health of teachers and young people but also the impact on schools and young people of shaking within the wider society.

The cumulative emotional impact of shaking can be more traumatic than that experienced by victims of one tragedy, such as a tragic loss or accident. In the latter, survivors have a specific event to 'blame' for the intensity of their 'felt' response and, with appropriate support will normally resume some semblance of normal life. The adage that 'time is a great healer' is relevant here. However, in the context of global shaking people experience persistent low level wounds to their sense of self, which leave them feeling undermined and often deskilled.

Repetitive change injury

Desensitisation is a key method of coping with the kind of repetitive change injury that is caused by endless change and the experience of being an 'I–It' in multiple contexts. I am not suggesting that all teachers or young people have cut off from their feelings or been irrevocably damaged by shaking. However, the high turnover of teachers and leaders and the dire plight of many schools in disadvantaged communities alluded to earlier point to failures in the system to protect leaders and teachers from the negative effects of change and to find humane ways of developing resilience and stamina within the school community as a whole.

The mental health statistics related to children and young people are indicative of a deterioration in the psychological health of children and young people and of a wider range of related behaviours. In 2003, 10%

of children were being treated for a serious mental health disorder (Meltzer et al., 2003) and 40,000 children in England were taking pre-scribed anti-depressants (Sunderland, 2004). More children and young people are engaging in forms of self-harm, such as binge drinking, sub-stance abuse or other-harm, as in bullying and street violence. Increas-ing numbers are presenting themselves to counselling helplines or organisations to seek support for a range of social and emotional prob-lems (Place2Be, 2006; Sunderland 2004).

The Mental Health Foundation report a 70% rise in anxiety and depressive disorders between 2001 and 2004. Research undertaken in Japan indicates that deliberate self-harm is a significant problem in early adolescence (Izutsu et al., 2006). In the UK over 170,000 people, mainly adolescents, are hospitalised for self-harming each year and the numbers are steadily rising (Sunderland, 2004). Suicide accounts for over one-fifth of all deaths in young people (Mind, 2006). Isolation/implosion on the one hand and domination/explosion on the other represent the polarised behaviours of children 'at risk'. The vast majority of children and young people move along this continuum in response to the field conditions in their classrooms, playgrounds, homes and community.

It is reasonable therefore to assume that most classrooms contain a proportion of young people who can be defined as 'at risk' in mental health terms and many more who may be acting out in a range of ways or suffering in silence and in isolation. Children with mental health problems are three times more likely than other children to have special educational needs (Meltzer et al., 2003) and therefore to need more than educational support to overcome their underlying difficulties. Certain individuals and groups attempt to navigate a way through the system without drawing too much negative attention to themselves. 'Silence' is often used, for example, to describe the relationship between sexuality and education and particularly reflects the taboo surrounding homosexuality in UK society and throughout much of the world (Bid-dulph, 2006). Many young people are therefore abandoned to sink or swim in a heterosexual hegemony that defines them as 'other' and therefore as shameful, with nowhere to discuss and process their vulnerability, nowhere to be accepted as valuable members of the school community. Lesbian, gay and bisexual young people are partic-ularly vulnerable to making suicide attempts and account for over half of all suicide attempts in this age group in the UK each year (D'Augelli et al., 2005).

If the purposes of education are to be concerned with more than cultural transmission, economic productivity and social reconstruction and if we are to keep competent but disheartened, disillusioned and exhausted teachers and leaders in education, then leadership of learning must address the psychological health needs of all members of the school community. However, given the pressures on the teaching profession for pupil outcomes and the 'deficit' construct of mental health within society it is understandable that teachers have resisted embracing health, and particularly mental health in schools, as one of the core purposes of schooling.

In other countries, such as Australia, Sweden and Denmark, considerable efforts are being made to develop a positive understanding of mental health issues in schools. Much of this work focuses on struggling or failing schools in deprived and disadvantaged communities where the tangible evidence of mental health problems is more easily discernible. Unfortunately, this practice colludes with the myth that pupils and teachers working in schools within the broad range of 'normal and successful' circumstances do not need to attend to mental health issues. This negativity only serves to discount, minimise and negate the distress, grief, anger and confusion that are hidden behind the statistics outlined above and that Freudians and existentialist philosophers believe to characterise the human condition (Freud 1915-17; Sartre, 1958). Freshwater and Robertson, (2002) contend that emotions are the 'Cinderella of the Psyche' and that individuals are starved of the emotional recognition and connection they crave. There is a strong emotional investment in perpetuating the lie that mental health problems are not an issue for each and every one of us on the planet.

The First International Conference on Promoting Health in Schools (Helsinki, 1999) claimed that mental health is integral to health in schools. Recently, the Government's Green Paper, 'Every Child Matters', and its legislative spine, the Children Act, 2004, acknowledge the vital role that schools can play in improving the well being of young people, particularly those deemed to be vulnerable and at risk.

New leadership?

This brief overview of the state of mental health of schools and communities provides some evidence of the effects of global and national change on education over several decades. A consumer led society encourages people to chase material goals and conform to a worldview that wealth, image and profession are all super-ordinate to personality, character and integrity. Affluenza (James, 2006), the widespread preoccupation with money, appearances, possessions and fame, contributes to and reflects the transitory nature of people's lives as they move jobs and change relationships in their quest for social acceptability and admiration. This affluenza virus is particularly prevalent in English-speaking nations and is directly linked with higher rates of mental illness, on average twice as high as in their non-English speaking counterparts.

Children and young people however, are the real victims of this human phenomenon. Whereas the children of working parents for example, used to be cared for by a blood relative or close neighbour, more and more babies and children are looked after in institutional settings as both parents choose to or have to go out to work and live away from their extended families. This loss of community ties is evidenced in the linked studies of Young and Wilmott (1957) and Dench et al., (2006) which highlight the demise of the extended family over the 50 year period between the studies. Young and old people live in isolation without the support or care of their family network. Even the most dedicated substitute carers cannot give babies and young children the amount of attention and stimulation they need. Moreover, staff turnover means that this vulnerable population may have a succession of key workers rather than one stable, consistent, loving adult throughout their early years. In this way, the baby and young child experience themselves as an 'It' both in the nursery and in the home, their emotional needs unattended to in ways that foster a strong sense of personal security, identity and self worth. Much of this emotional neglect is unintentional and yet it is highly symptomatic of the shaking and of the resulting fragmentation and destruction of families, communities and societies.

In 2004 25% of children grew up in single parent families (ONS, 2006) and more in reconstituted families with step-parents and step-siblings. The 'normal' and ubiquitous emotional 'storm and stress' of contemporary childhood, whether caused by lack of quality time with parents, or adjustment and loss issues (such as family illness/death, parental separation, new/successive adult parent substitutes) may individually or in combination contribute to repetitive change injury. Similarly, more materialistic preoccupations, interpersonal rivalries and games of domination and submission are ever present in the undertow of school life and serve to preoccupy young people's attention, many of whom feel doubly neglected and/or punished within a school system that is experienced as more interested in their contribution to the school's reputation and positioning in the school league tables than to their personal, social, emotional and intellectual development as the citizens of tomorrow.

As highlighted at the start of this chapter, many young people struggle against the odds to find a way through the daily trauma of survival in communities where substance addiction, crime, gang warfare and community violence represent maladaptive ways of coping with the overwhelming feelings evoked by multiple deprivation, social invisibility and hopelessness. Young people in our schools are already suffering their own repetitive change injury. Coping with constant unpredictability and fear of social, emotional, physical abuse or annihilation comes at a price. Having lost touch with their own feelings, too many young people are able to tune out to the feelings of others, including teachers and engage in a 'game' of tormenting and bullying others. Even the best intentioned and most committed teachers find the volume and range of maladaptive behaviours impossible to deal with and experience feelings of intense failure as their efforts to teach the prescribed curriculum are so blatantly sabotaged (Lupton, 2005).

So what are the implications of all this for leadership? If children and young people are to achieve and to actively participate in society then this internalised 'I–It' process must be challenged within the education system. According to Kasser (2002) the processes described above have contributed to the neglect of four fundamental human needs, namely the need:

- for security

- for intimacy and relatedness

- to feel competent and effective

- to be authentic, autonomous and playful.

If schools are to address these needs and limit further damage to mental health and well being, they need leadership that promotes a more constructive view of self, self-in-relationship and self-in-community.

It could be argued that a litmus test of effective emotional leadership is the extent to which teachers take control of their own sphere of influence. Breaking the cycle of negative emotions, thoughts and behaviours that are prevalent in many classrooms might involve, for example, seeking new ways of engaging with students and parents that honour and respect their reality and their truth. In other words, teachers can heal themselves, support pupils' learning and take back control of the educational agenda within their school to co-create new field conditions appropriate to their particular context. Such teachers are leaders of learning (Harris and Muijs, 2005; Durrant and Holden, 2006). Teacher leadership has become the 'growing edge' of educational leadership theory in recent years (Spillane, 2006; Harris, 2006). This literature focuses on the overt forms of teacher leadership, such as sharing tasks and greater involvement of teachers in decision making. Shared forms of leadership must, however, also attend to the emotional domain and ensure that the emotional (over)load is more evenly distributed. Whilst there is some recognition of the need for shared emotional work in schools (Beatty, 2000; Ackerman and Maslin-Ostrowski, 2004; Beatty and Brew, 2004; Durrant and Holden, 2006) there is a need for greater understanding about how to achieve this. New forms of shared emotional leadership may go some way to reducing the isolation of formal leaders and deepening the quality of contact and relatedness between formal leaders and teacher leaders. The following chapter will outline the emotional terrain of leadership in schools as a prelude to introducing the empirical data on the emotional work of leadership.

Endnote

[1] I am appreciative of the UKCP Professional Conference (Cambridge, July 2006) organisers for the concept of shaking and for this quotation.

3 *The emotional work of school leadership*

Introduction

When Pat took over as head teacher of Meway Comprehensive School (11–16) the staff were still reeling from the shock of their Ofsted inspection which identified serious weaknesses in the quality of teaching in many areas of the school. In former times Meway had sustained a strong reputation as a 'good school' and competition for places had been fierce. Middle class parents had bussed or driven their children to school from all over the city. However, during the previous decade changes in local housing, employment and public transport contributed to the school's changing fortunes and middle class parents began to move their children elsewhere. Pat found her staff highly resistant to everything she proposed, blaming their predicament on the new breed of pupils and parents they had to 'deal with'. A collective form of low self esteem and hopelessness pervaded the school, draining energy and joy from relationships and from the process of learning.

With support from a leadership coach Pat was able to see beyond the presenting defensiveness and blame culture and recognise the underlying vulnerability of her staff, many of whom were grieving for the 'good old days' when they had been a successful and thriving school and for the head teacher that had protected them and made them feel 'special'. By contrast she knew that, having arrived in the school hot on the tails of the Ofsted judgement, she was not welcome and perceived as an intruder who could not possibly understand the difficulties they faced. Conscious of their collective sense of shame and related defensiveness, Pat recognised that developing 'emotional fitness' would be the first stepping stone on a long journey towards 'emotional alchemy', a way of relating that engages and enriches teachers and students in powerful, deep learning (Harris, 2004).

Pat had learned this from her experience as deputy head of a large upper school (14–18 years) in a leafy suburb where teachers had resisted the categorisation of the school as 'cruising' and been equally reluctant to change. She understands intuitively that leading change is a bit like navigating a path through an emotional minefield. No amount of strategic planning or rationality can predict the impact of others' responses to change initiatives. Fragile emotions can erupt into tears of distress, outbursts of righteous anger or implode as in shame and depression.

What resources will Pat need to work with this climate of negativity? How can she support colleagues and pupils to move towards more response-able emotional engagement and institutional well being? What leadership will this process demand of her and of others in the school community in order to move the school onto a positive emotional trajectory where learning and relating are vibrant, energising and humanising?

The emotional climate of change

> It is the quality of fragility, the capacity for being 'shaken up', that paradoxically is the key to growth. (Dossey, 1982: 84)

Teaching is essentially emotional in nature (Salzberger-Wittenberg et al., 1983) and therefore 'highly charged with feeling, aroused by and directed towards not just people but also values and ideals' (Nias, 1996: 293). Good teaching and positive emotion go hand in hand. There is a substantial body of evidence to suggest that cognition and emotion are as inseparable as night and day (Le Doux, 1998; Damasio 1999) and combine together in social practices in complex ways (Greenhalgh, 1994 ; Greenberg et al., 1993). A positive mood at the time of learning, for example, enhances both learning of content (Gilligan & Bower, 1984) and subsequent recall (Blaney, 1986).

> As an emotional practice teaching activates, colours and expresses the feelings and actions of teachers and those they influence. All teaching is therefore inextricably emotional, either by design or default. Teachers can enthuse their students or bore them. (Hargreaves, 2001: 1057)

It is not surprising therefore that students describe effective teachers as likeable (Aspy and Roebuck, 1977; Kohl, 1994) and experience their classes as stimulating, challenging and joyful places to be. In this sense every teacher is a leader of learning and has a responsibility to ensure that the emotional climate in their classroom is conducive to student engagement in learning. Such emotional practice may be described as an act of love. Indeed, Liston and Garrison (2004) identify love as integral to good pedagogy and Freire (1995) goes so far as to assert that teaching is not possible without the courage to love. However, this does assume the student's capacity to accept and take in the teacher's love as a genuine source of emotional and intellectual nourishment. Perhaps it is more accurate to say it is impossible to teach effectively without the courage to communicate love and the persistence to convey this message to those hardest to reach.

The emotional landscapes of teaching are shaped by social, political and institutional realities, which interact for better or worse with the love, passion and sense of moral purpose that motivate teachers' work. In separate studies, Nias (1996) and Halton (1995) identify a range of deeply disturbing emotions, such as hostility, mistrust, fear and despair in education and attribute these directly to the effects of structural change in schools. Carlyle and Woods (2002) study of the emotions of teacher stress identifies not only the human loss of those teachers who are diagnosed with chronic stress and burnout but also the waste of emotional energy of stressed teachers who bravely soldier on.

There is little doubt that teacher 'dis'-stress will unwittingly be communicated to students. In this atmosphere safety is compromised and students' capacity for learning impeded. This appears to be the case at Meway where, rather than rising to the challenges of changing circumstances, the school has continued to function according to time honoured ways, a characteristic which often leads to diminished results, frustration and increasing cynicism (Gentile, 1996; Guskey, 1997). It is little wonder that the school is suddenly drowning in a sea of previously repressed emotions. Love, passion and moral purpose are conspicuous by their absence whilst despondency, despair and anger are in abundance. The task ahead of Pat and her staff is therefore a daunting one and it will be necessary first and foremost to establish the emotional conditions within which personal and social healing and renewal can flourish. She will need to establish emotional fitness for purpose.

Emotional fitness

It is now quite clear that the actualisation of the highest human potentials is possible … on a mass basis … only under 'good conditions'. Or more directly, good human beings will generally need a good society in which to grow. (Maslow, 1971: 7)

Socially generated 'dis'-ease and the associated lack of well being (James, 2006) requires socially generated solutions in which individuals and groups can grow into their potential. Given conditions in the field it is understandable that many teachers, pupils and communities feel a sense of hopelessness. It will take much more than organisational and classroom level change to engage the hearts and minds of disaffected teachers and pupils.

In some schools there will inevitably be pockets of underperformance but that does not mean all teachers underperform. Some committed teachers in these circumstances may take excessive responsibility and find themselves acting as emotional conduits for unacknowledged and unexpressed emotionality within school, such as resentment towards colleagues who do not contribute to the common good or envy towards an 'outstanding' colleague or department. Sensitive to these emotional dynamics such teachers can easily become overwhelmed. If, for example, they turn this negativity in on themselves they may experience a crisis of personal identity and self efficacy and need the professional support of a mentor, coach or counsellor to help them regain perspective. When the identity of the whole school is under threat, as at Meway, then this crisis of identity is multiplied and teachers share the collective experience of fragility and shame, even though some may be adept at concealing it behind anger, frustration or a brave face.

It is precisely at these moments of fragility, however, that old patterns and ways of being can be relaxed and let go of or clung onto like driftwood. Beisser (1970), a gestalt psychotherapist, coined this phenomenon the 'paradoxical nature of change'. His research and clinical practice led him to theorise that real change occurs when people stop resisting or chasing change and truly accept the reality of what 'is'. It is the acceptance of what 'is' that loosens constructs and enables new learning to occur. He notes that the more people try to change the more elusive change becomes. In a not dissimilar vein but from an educational perspective, Joyce (1982) notes the importance of 'dynamic disequilibrium' to promote profound learning and change. Being disturbed and also feeling the extent of the disturbance acts as a catalyst for new learning to occur. Both of these perspectives have profound implications for the leadership of change.

The existing research base of School Improvement demonstrates the limits of conventional forms of change and development to bring about sustainable improvement. Sustainability is particularly challenging in those schools that struggle to recruit and retain head teachers. Disaffection and the emotional distress of teachers and students can be compounded in such schools unless strategies and systems have been developed to ensure minimal disruption during periods of high staff turnover and changes in leadership (Hargreaves and Fink, 2003). Equally, government policies can serve to pit one school against another and seduce middle class students and high calibre teachers to move to more successful and well resourced schools with dire effects on the emotional well being and education of those left behind (Tomlinson, 2006) including school leaders:

> The emotional health of leaders is a scarce environmental resource. Leadership that drains its leaders dry is not leadership that will last. Unless reformers and policy-makers care for leaders' personal and professional selves, they will engineer short-term gains only by mortgaging the entire future of leadership. (Hargreaves and Fink, 2003: 8)

Emotional resilience must therefore be seen as far more than a competence to be nurtured in individuals. If one of the purposes of education is to effect a more humane society, then change is needed in the individual and collective psyche of schools and communities. School transformation and human transformation are two sides of the same coin and it falls upon those in formal leadership roles to generate the energy and will necessary to engage in and effect school change.

In the early stages of school-based change the impetus is normally driven by external pressures, as is the case at Meway. The negative pressures this creates on particular schools is compounded by the negative attitudes towards teachers embedded in government policies and manifest in dysfunctional relationships between some parents, pupils and their teachers (Hargreaves, 2000, 2001). Formal leaders may experience collective pressure to find quick, easy answers to the school's problems which do not involve personal change or institutional growth. In these instances the change process itself is viewed as an 'It' and emphasis is placed upon the task of restructuring systems, procedures, policies and teams. Whilst these may save time and paper and raise the self esteem of those that created them, such strategies rarely get to the heart of the problem. More importantly they fail to raise collective self esteem by engaging colleagues in the resolution of shared problems, or to harness their leadership potential. Instead, they create an ambivalent culture of mistrust on the one hand and dependency on the other.

Unless supported to understand the problems they face, staff feel resentful of initiatives that demand of their time and energy and also mistrust the leader's motives. It is not unusual for people in such distress to long for someone to rescue them. There is however, no fairy godmother on the horizon to save teachers from government reform. Instead, developing emotional fitness for purpose serves to stem the flow of toxic negativity by re-humanising schools. Raising self esteem, developing community, restoring hope and building morale are interrelated facets of this process. Such transformative organisational change, however, can only occur when teachers also take responsibility for their part in developing school culture and recognise that organisational growth is not sustainable unless accompanied by the personal growth and transformation of community members. Effecting change is perceived here as a two-way process involving mutual respect, care and honesty. Ambiguity, dissonance and difference are not just tolerated but also understood to positively contribute to trust and collective ownership of the school's well being:

> When fears, anxieties and even resistance are articulated and accepted as normal and healthy responses to change, teachers are more likely to trust that their efforts will not be ridiculed or dismissed. Communication and positive relationships are central components of emotional fitness allowing staff to realistically assess and confront their own strengths and weaknesses in order to achieve personal growth and change. (Harris, 2004: 402)

Developing emotional fitness is premised therefore on the concurrent development of emotional literacy. The personal and professional learning arising from emotional engagement in the processes of change is supportive of building leadership capacity in teachers and students. In this way some of the emotional as well as task-based work of leadership can be shared. If Pat can generate this at Meway, she will increase her chance of surviving and the school's chance of thriving.

Emotional literacy

Extensive research in the field of counselling and psychotherapy points to the significance of the therapeutic relationship in creating the conditions for personal change (Hubble et al., 1999). Carl Rogers' pioneering research (1968) into counselling practice in institutional settings led him to identify six conditions which he believed to be necessary and sufficient to establish a therapeutic alliance. The three 'core conditions' are often cited as essential in enabling people to feel safe enough to communicate feelings of vulnerability and fear. It is the counsellor's capacity to accept and honour the individual's personal experience that releases the 'client' to fully feel their emotions, accept them and let them go. In doing so the client owns and takes responsibility for their experience. This is the paradoxical nature of change as it is experienced in relationship.

Such relationships gradually enable individuals to emerge from the emotional isolation of their defensiveness, show their true feelings and experience the newness of being accepted, affirmed and appreciated for their difference, rather than judged, labelled and ostracised. This order of relationship is therefore important for the development of school communities in which people feel safe enough to learn and grow. Wenger et al., (2002) talk of an 'aliveness' that can emerge within community members as the relational conditions support authenticity between people leading to greater trust in the community and in the processes of change. Whilst the work of Carl Rogers (1951) is helpful in supporting the development of effective relationships in the majority, there are many children within the school community for whom Rogers' core conditions are necessary but not sufficient. Wetz's (2006) narrative study of 16 year old youths leaving Bristol mainstream schools without any qualifications highlights the complexities of young people's lives as they struggle with multiple experiences of isolation, loss, discontinuity and inconsistent, unreliable support in both family and school settings.

Research into child development (Stern, 1985) is supported by research into the child's developing brain (Schore, 1994) and highlights the importance of affirming, attuned, consistent and stimulating relationships for healthy brain development and for an internalised sense of safety and security in children. In the absence of such experiences a young person's emotional brain development is impaired and their experience of neglect and abandonment intense. If caregivers are also regularly abusive towards children then there may be severe negative consequences for a young person's capacity to tolerate anxiety or distress and to engage in learning (Schore, 1994; Gerhardt, 2004).

Bowlby's (1988) attachment theory provides a framework for understanding the importance of a 'secure base' (Holmes, 2001) for insecurely attached young people who defend against perceived attacks on the 'self' by attacking others either verbally, physically or both. Patterns of relationships and the organisation of classroom conditions (for example, the nomadic experience of young people in schools as they move from class to class; unsupervised break times) can exacerbate early trauma and trigger challenging behaviour patterns in young people who do not have the means by which to self-soothe and manage their anxiety (Bowlby, 1988). Whilst emotional deficits in the child's experience with primary caregivers cannot be compensated for, teachers can learn ways of relating to children and young people that are more emotionally attuned and offer a different, potentially reparative experience of relationship with adults. When pupils feel visible and cared for, they believe they matter and this can make a real difference to their willingness to engage with learning (Harris, Vincent et al., 2006).

The role of those in formal leadership positions therefore is to create a school which can act as a secure base for insecurely attached children (and staff!). Many insecurely attached children survive primary education because of the predictability of the school day and the consistency of relationship with a form tutor. There is some evidence to suggest that the transition to secondary school is particularly traumatic for these young people and that in the absence of a secure base they exclude themselves (Wetz, 2006) or are excluded (Harris, Vincent et al., 2006). School merely intensifies their emotional wounds and their beliefs that they are worthless and unlovable.

Stefan Karpman (1968) coined the term 'drama triangle' as a way of helping individuals make sense of personal experience and particularly of personally challenging situations or 'dramas' between people. Most educators would recognise a dramatic element as one reality of living in a community whether in classrooms, staffrooms or other communal spaces. The triangle is therefore primarily a tool for self awareness and a means by which individuals can reflect on the roles they take up in relationship with others and make personal choices about subsequent behaviour. It is a model that I have shared with many teachers and leaders and which they have reported as a useful and powerful aide to reflection on their professional and personal lives. (See Figure 3.1). Karpman identifies three positions that inhibit effective relationships, namely the persecutor (as in authoritarian, aggressive, domineering), the victim (the recipient who feels chasitised, humiliated, dismissed by the other) and the rescuer (who tries to smooth things over and make everything alright for one or both parties).

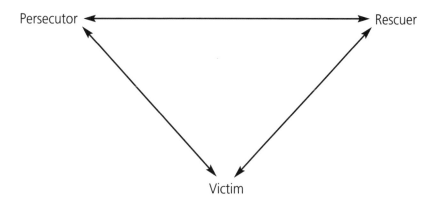

Figure 3.1: Karpman's Drama Triangle

Whenever communication involves people taking up one or more positions on the triangle, then an authentic relationship is unlikely. Furthermore, switches in these roles and their related existential positions make for great drama, high emotion, surges of stress hormones – and much unhappiness. Such interpersonal dynamics compromise the development of emotional literacy and often lead individuals to feel wounded and stuck, unable to effect change in their environment.

Exercise

Persecutor makes others suffer – punishes, shames

Rescuer makes others feel better – takes over, placates

Victim acts helpless, unable to resolve the situation – does not take responsibility

Think of your relationships in school. Which of these positions are you most likely to take up when under stress? Make some notes for yourself.

If we view teaching through a broader, more contextualised view of emotion we can become sensitised to the darker emotions in teaching such as guilt, shame, anger, jealousy, frustration and fear (Fineman, 1993). Only a few studies explore the underlying emotional dynamics of school leaders' work. The concept of wounding in schools has been examined by Blase and Blase (2003) who identified three levels of mis-treatment/abuse of teachers by school leaders. These ranged from indirect and moderately aggressive behaviours, (Level One) to direct and severely aggressive behaviours (Level Three). Wounding leaders are found to induce feelings of fear, anger, depression and isolation in their victims. In similar vein, Ackerman and Maslin-Ostrowski's (2004) research on school leaders recognises a thin line between wounding and wounded leaders, a line that can be easily crossed where there is an absence of emotional awareness and understanding of self. They also identify the experience of leadership wounding as an 'important source of emotional and social learning, and a critical opening to the exercise of leadership' (Maslin-Ostrowski and Ackerman, 2000).

> The courage to learn such things, it seems to us, is among the most pressing challenges school teachers and leaders share today. (Ackerman and Maslin-Ostrowski, 2004: 313)

Borrowing Freire's assertion, leadership, like teaching, is impossible without the courage to learn, the courage to love and the courage to persist until one's love is accepted and trusted. If leaders are to ensure that they avoid wounding others and survive being wounded by others, then they need to become aware of their own emotional needs and of the ways in which their personal and professional story may affect their capacity to facilitate and co-create effective change processes.

In an emotionally literate school there will be a critical mass of people, including students, who have enough emotional literacy and wisdom to recognise a wounding drama in action and find ways of being or supporting others that change the field. Choy's (1990) 'Winner's Triangle' is helpful here. She presents three alternative posi-tions to those of Karpman, namely Assertive (vs Persecutor), Caring (vs Rescuer) and Vulnerable (vs Victim), to interrupt the drama, or game between individuals. I have adapted her model slightly in order to keep the initials, P, V and R, and to preserve the sense of movement or flow between the positions. Here, individuals take personal agency without oppressing or playing games with others. Rather than moving into victim role, individuals own their vulnerability in specific situations and reach out to others who are able to respond without rescuing but with due respect and care for the agency of the other and their capacity to find their own solutions to difficulties.

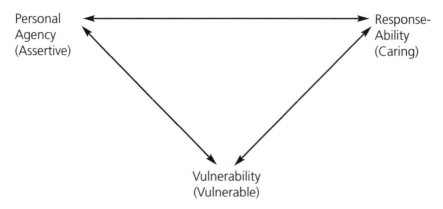

Figure 3.2: Adapted from Choy (1990) 'The Winner's Triangle'

Awareness of self can therefore be seen as the sine qua non of good teaching and sound leadership. Without it we have no compass by which to guide our actions. Fritz Perls, the co-founder of gestalt psychotherapy, highlights the key role of awareness of our emotions and deems this to be central to healthy functioning:

> It is only through the recognition of your emotions that you can be aware, as a biological organism, either of what you are up against in the environment, or of what special opportunities are at the moment presented. It is only if you accept your longing for someone or something … that you obtain orientation for appropriate action. (Perls et al., 1951: 98–9)

Like teaching, leadership is always, although not solely, an emotional practice and is infused with love, care and compassion for pupils' lives and achievements, for teachers' lives and professional development and for the well being of the total community. Leadership work is hard emotional labour (Hochschild, 1983) especially when fuelled by love and a commitment to integrity and/or when the school faces extremely challenging circumstances, whether by dint of its location or some human tragedy. Although many of these circumstances, such as unemployment and poor housing or the murder of an adult or child are beyond the direct influence of the school, they bear heavily on school life as children and young people transport the distress or despair of their community into school. They need to be met by adults whose words and actions are suffused with generosity, patience, care and a willingness to be moved, perhaps even changed by their involvement with the young person.

It is therefore essential to ensure a balance between emotional giving and self care. Otherwise there is a risk of treating the self as an 'It' and setting an 'I–It' precedent for intrapersonal and interpersonal relationships within the school. It is lonely at the top and it is therefore imperative that appropriate systems are in place to keep the leader connected to humanity and to the humanity and care of others.

Developing emotional fitness and literacy is not a one-off task – it is about creating a climate in which people feel safe enough to learn and grow into their capacity to value themselves and others, to relate effectively and to lead. However, if relationships are to feel equal, as opposed to unequal (power/status led), and individuals are to be encouraged to contribute to emotional leadership then more emotionally self-disclosing and probing forms of relating will have to be developed. The primary skill involved is the capacity to be aware of self in the moment-by-moment experience of relating with another and to take full responsibility for one's own experience. In this way every contact is a journey into the unknown and is potentially full of surprises. It is the extent to which people can engage in this kind of relating that determines how far new realities can be co-created between stakeholders. Peer observation, peer counselling, mentoring and coaching are potential vehicles for developing the practice of leadership, particularly if they model authentic ways of being contactful and present.

Every school has challenging colleagues, people for example, who appear to be driven by a destructive emotional agenda and gain gratuitous pleasure in deliberately sabotaging meetings and new initiatives. They can have a powerful negative effect on trust and community building and need to be challenged appropriately. Having examined more emotionally attuned ways of relating with and engaging individual colleagues, this emotional practice needs to be extended and deepened to support leadership of learning throughout the school.

Emotional maintenance and depth

The process of transforming a school is dependent on the capacity to transform school culture, the shared values, understandings and ways of being that enable people to develop a sense of belonging and place in the total institution. School cultures have their own unique rhythm, colour and pace, and smaller units within the total institution, such as departmental teams and year groups, will have their own mini cultures that can be symbiotic or discordant with the larger institutional culture. It is proposed that, rather than attempting to change discordant cultures to 'fit in' with the dominant culture, a transformational school will welcome differences and view their potential as agents for rich, stimulating conversations about what matters to people in school and how they can work together to resolve differences without enforcing conformity. Such experiential lessons are essential for an inclusive school and equip people with key skills in managing difference and negotiating 'win/win' ways through complex problems and dilemmas and diverse cultural perspectives. Such skills are equally necessary within the context of extended schools. Internal differences and mini cultures may be compounded by closer relationships with other helping professionals (for example counsellors, social workers, health visitors), whose perspectives, priorities, values and ways of engaging with children and young people may not sit comfortably with school norms, roles, structures and systems.

It is inevitable that a school that is striving to become more emotionally aware and attuned to the needs of individuals and groups will demand no small measure of personal growth from its community members. New forms and patterns of personal and social relations may be required to break negative patterns of perceiving, thinking and behaving. It is the task of the leader to model and embody a way of being and relating that simultaneously respects, honours and responds to the distress of teachers whilst holding a spotlight on the core purpose of education, the effective learning and well being of students.

Organisational change involves the capacity to engage with inter-personal and inter-group processes in ways that deepen awareness and understanding of self and of self-in-relationship. This is particularly important in schools where hierarchical structures can legitimise the use of formal power to disempower colleagues and young people. Young people, for example, tend to be astute in their evaluations of teachers and yet this information is rarely accessed to support the development of awareness and insight in teachers. MacBeath (2006), however, found that students were more measured and sensitive in their feedback about teachers than teachers had imagined or given them credit for. When teachers open themselves up to feedback from colleagues and students, they are more likely to reflect on habitual ways of perceiving the self/understanding events and recognise the existence of choice. Emotional depth is achieved when individuals feel safe enough to share their vulnerabilities and their achievements and are able to acknowledge and respond empathically to these in others. Peer observation, peer mentoring, student/teacher cooperative learning and student-led research can all be powerful ways of deepening relationships and simultaneously deepening awareness of practice.

Attending to emotional safety is therefore an important aspect of developing emotional fitness. Teachers cannot be expected to be real with one another and tell 'their truth' if they are concerned about how such information might be used against them. In today's challenging circumstances a trusting environment is facilitated in the first instance by the tone the leader sets for relationships. The ability of the leader to respond to the negative emotions of staff, to offer appropriate support to soothe anxieties, and challenge to stimulate honest exploration of difficult and sensitive issues, kick starts the process of reculturing and creating a climate of trust. In time individuals may feel more willing to support and challenge each other and engage in creative conflict. Such experiential learning develops a sense of individual and collective responsibility to one another and for the well being of the school community (Harris and Biddulph, 2000) and is therefore an important aspect of building leadership capacity amongst a range of colleagues across the school. All these interactions need to occur within a framework of compassionate care for all and of moral concern for the quality of student learning. Taking greater responsibility for student learning and for teacher student relationships is fraught with risks to self esteem and self identity. However, interactions with colleagues and direct work-related experiences can be influential in forging new identities (Busher, 2005). Therefore a supportive and non-judgmental climate is essential to contain the emotional anxiety involved in personal growth (Rogers, 1992).

Making mistakes is a normal and healthy part of learning and it is imperative that mistakes can be shared openly if they are to contribute to deeper learning and personal meaning. Although benign humour has been proven to be highly effective in building collegiality (Terrion and Ashforth, 2002), the absence of humour in some staffrooms and classrooms may be more indicative of field conditions than of a lack of desire for fun or relationship. Just as positive mood affects learning, so it can affect change processes and act as glue in the process of emotional bonding.

Real transformation of schools, however, does not stop at healing relationships. Transforming humans involves a commitment to self actualisation, not as a goal, in the way that Maslow presented it in his hierarchy of needs (1970) but as a process of moment-by-moment change. If human transformation is concerned with progress towards a more humane society then it follows that developing the leadership capacity of all is essential. By leadership I am referring to the capacity and willingness of each person to take responsibility for their own lives and for their contribution to the common good.

> Leadership is not the private reserve of a few charismatic men and women. It is a process that ordinary people use when they are bringing forth the best in themselves and others. (Kouzes and Posner, 2000 cited in Kouzes and Posner, 2003: 324)

Teacher leadership of learning only makes sense, therefore, within the context of student leadership of learning. Mobilising and engaging with student 'voice' is presented as one way of supporting leadership development in young people. Student voice that eschews tokenism can change the relationship between teachers and learners and be a launch pad for more co-creative and enriching learning between students and teachers. The same is true for parents and governors. An initial response to this might be one of feeling overwhelmed or somewhat cynical about the prospect of truly engaging such potentially disparate voices in the development of the school. However, from a field theoretical perspective every new encounter and contribution to the total field has an effect that is greater than the sum of its parts. Taking responsibility for self and for the common good supports the development of a collaborative 'We' culture, in which overlapping spheres of influence and involvement contribute to a shared sense of belonging and moral purpose. In this form teacher leadership, student leadership and formal leadership weave together to create rich learning environments characterised by genuine participation, respectful dialogue and experimentation in teaching and learning. Emotionally deep relationships also contribute to the refinement of emotional competence (Hall et al., 1999) and help promote positive affect and well being throughout the school (Ciarrochi & Scott, 2006).

4 *Developing emotional awareness*

Introduction

Chris was appointed as head of English in a large comprehensive school following the retirement of her predecessor, a quiet, calm and committed teacher with sound organisational skills. Having just completed a Masters in Educational Leadership, Chris had relished the prospect of building up the English department, which in her view needed more dynamic leadership and an injection of energy and creativity. She was committed to offering students exciting, interactive ways of learning and, although a little overwhelmed by her at first, her team members were interested in learning about and developing new approaches to teaching the subject. They found her enthusiasm infectious. She organised visits to galleries and museums to promote awareness of different ways of seeing and representing the world and to encourage students to explore their own relationship to these different media and to develop their own creative forms of self expression. Staff actively supported her in preparing for the trips and took turns in accompanying her. Year 10 and 11 students wrote up their experiences and, facilitated by Chris, developed these into a 'performance', which they presented to Lower School students, governors and parents towards the end of the autumn term. Several 'challenging' students were actively involved and gave creditable performances much to the surprise of many of the school staff, students and parents. Chris was proving herself to be an effective teacher leader.

In the spring term Chris introduced a simple numerical student evaluation of lesson pro-forma within the department. The data was collated and used to inform discussions about teaching and learning and lesson planning within the team. The data soon showed that Chris's scores were significantly higher than those of her team members.

Around the same time team colleagues began to experience some mild hostility from students who asked to be moved to Chris's teaching groups. The team challenged her decision to move two such students and voiced their concerns about the impact on them and on their classes. Chris dismissed these, viewing them as symptomatic of team envy due to her popularity and competence. Soon, however, a few students complained of being unfairly treated and accused her of favouritism. Chris responded by giving them some extra group time after school to support their English course work.

Chris's colleagues appealed to the head teacher who, anxious not to alienate such a popular and creative teacher, also dismissed their concerns and agreed with Chris's interpretation of their motivations. One year later Chris left the school to take up an assistant principal post at a nearby school. That summer the English department's SATs and GCSE results were lower than expected, leaving a potential problem for Chris's successor.

Whilst Chris's personal engagement and commitment to her students was high she had little awareness of, interest in or concern for her colleagues or for the impact of her behaviour on them. Chris's lack of care for and responsibility towards her own staff reflects an inflated view of self. Chris sets herself up as special and superior to her colleagues and makes sure that she maintains that position by subtly undermining and demoralising her staff team. By accusing them of professional jealousy she effectively disempowers them and discredits them in the eyes of the head teacher and other senior staff. They become seen as a 'problem' which has to be managed.

Chris's genuine passion for teaching and her creativity have much potential to effect good in the school. However, she is hampered by a stunning lack of awareness of her own internal process and of the way in which her needs, fears and vulnerabilities have been buried and overlaid by a false self. This presenting adult self is reliant on achievement, a sense of perfectionism and omnipotence to feel okay. Chris therefore projects her own envy, competitiveness and worthlessness onto her colleagues. Although motivated by a desire to enhance the student experience, Chris creates an environmental field in which students and senior management become dependent on her and colleagues start to feel and act as if they actually are worthless. In reality, Chris's interpersonal need for attention, acceptance and affection is the primary motivating factor and, on the surface at least, it appears that she is successful in ensuring her needs are met. However, over time, Chris will find herself more and more isolated from her colleagues, whose needs she has systematically overlooked. Rather than face the pain of recognising and facing this abusive aspect of self, Chris may maintain her self-deception citing her colleagues 'envy' of her as an excuse to move to a new school, where she will repeat the cycle of seduction and disillusionment. This pattern may continue unabated for years.

It is also likely that Chris is extremely sensitive to slight or criticism, prone to depression and bothered by thoughts of worthlessness and imperfection. Most of the time however, she will work hard to disavow such experiences and maintain her false presenting self (Johnson, 1987). Had the head teacher listened to her colleagues and challenged her assertions and actions rather than colluding with her sense of specialness, Chris may have had cause to reflect on herself. Unfortunately, it may take a personal or professional crisis, stress or burnout before Chris is able to acknowledge that she has a problem. Chris believes that one charismatic teacher can make a charismatic school. In fact the opposite is true. Charisma is mere vanity unless it is used to inspire and support the growth of colleagues and students, to build a sense of community and energise people to work together for the common good.

Chris's story serves to highlight the significance of self awareness for effective leadership. Of course the majority of leaders are not as self-involved as Chris. They may just as easily however, be self negligent and put the needs of the school before themselves, leaving themselves depleted, or self abusive in that they overwork to the point of making themselves ill. In schools in challenging circumstances they may carry the emotional distress of parents, community and staff who feel constantly threatened by poverty, unemployment, violence or the threat of school closure. They may have to repress their own feelings in order to emotionally support colleagues, pupils and parents in the event of a traumatic death or event. They may feel they have to be approachable, warm and supportive even though they feel lonely and unsupported, or they are suffering some distress in their own life. They may have to support one colleague whose partner is dying, or discipline another who is underperforming and struggling with a messy divorce, punish or exclude a challenging child who they know to be 'at risk'. All of these are the day-to-day reality of people leadership and all of these are potentially stressful and emotionally draining experiences. In the midst of all of this they are charged with the responsibility for creating a welcoming, positive, achievement-focused and people-centred school or classroom environment and ethos.

In addition, the leaders whose voices are presented in this book face a daunting set of conflicting demands including overseeing the design and construction of a new school building, health and safety issues, school amalgamation and re-structuring, balancing the school's budget and managing the boundary between the school and the community, the local authority and the government.

It is argued here that leaders need to be able not only to survive the daily dramas and demands of the school and environment field but also to use them to further their own personal and professional growth and enhance their leadership capabilities. Despite being tragic, irritating, exasperating and often isolating experiences they are essential hurdles on the personal journey towards authentic, potent leadership. Unless leaders are able to engage with these emotional, cognitive and behavioural challenges their leadership remains a superficial, bureaucratic and essentially ineffective activity.

Leadership: being and doing

While there is no magical theory or emotional toolkit to solve any of these intractable problems, there are interpersonal skills and effective ways of building relationships, which can be learned and developed. However, such skills are worthless unless there is a coherent and credible 'fit' between the outer presentation of self and the inner world of thoughts and feelings. Effective leaders know, for example, how their own personal limitations can be projected onto others so that specific individuals, groups or teams are viewed as 'difficult' or 'bad', whilst others, often those who are most similar to and confluent with the leader are viewed as 'helpful' and 'good' people. They recognise how easy it is to create a climate in which people feel labelled and trapped in boxes of the leadership's making. Such leaders have an authority that is based on a deep understanding of self, a strong sense of identity and a degree of self acceptance that enables them to move beyond their ego and take an aerial overview of the school – of the ways in which people, policies and practice intersect and interact within the specific field conditions at that point in time. This inner strength and wider perspective help leaders to hold steady in difficult waters and ride any waves of discontent, resistance and sabotage as staff, governors, parents and pupils struggle with their own sense of fragility and their issues with authority and personal power, much of which may be outside their awareness at that point in time.

The leader that has embarked on their own inner journey has a deep understanding of the emotional distress and sense of loss involved in personal change. They are therefore more compassionate and able to connect with others as unique and special individuals rather than to judge them, berate them or cast them as a 'problem'. They create a sense of safety, consistency and care that enables others to work through their resistances and blocks and develop their own leadership capacities. Such leadership is a way of *being* and not just a way of doing.

Bennis' (2003) research and Loader's (1997) personal account of school leadership highlight the key role of self knowledge in developing an effective way of being as a leader. New ways of perceiving and leading are needed to make sense of the interconnected web of activity and relationships that are the engine of school life and that make the policies, procedures and tasks run more or less smoothly.

Self awareness and self knowledge

Committed leaders grow into their role and view it as an experiential learning journey which demands a degree of rigorous self honesty and soul searching and a willingness to befriend the multiple selves that constitute their personality. While it may be easy to embrace culturally acceptable selves, such as the social self, the fun self and the clever self, it is equally important to become intimately acquainted with the more neglected aspects of self, such as the vulnerable self that is hidden behind learned defences and the shadow self (Jung and von Franz, 1964) that is often denied until it erupts in protest at times of stress to damage self and others. Such deep work requires the support of others who are willing to offer constructive, honest feedback on behaviour and therefore stretch the leader to develop more insight about their blind spots and the impact of their way of being on others. However, it is the responsibility of the leader to integrate all their different selves and to recognise that real authority comes from within.

The journey into and through leadership is one of learning to be true to the self and to take full responsibility for *how* the school or classroom narrative is co-authored. If leaders are to pursue what is in the best interests of the school and community rather than what is in the best interests of personal identity and ambition, then self awareness and self knowledge are the foundations underpinning their work.

Awareness in action

David Loader's (1997) book *The Inner Principal* begins with an account of the day when his resignation was announced to the staff of Methodist Ladies College after 15 years as principal. During this event he found himself reflecting on how staff might be receiving the news.

> I felt a freeing of responsibility for the College. It was in good hands. I was not needed. Discharged of this responsibility for the College I looked around the staff and wondered what are they thinking and feeling. Then I made a personal jump. I asked myself: 'What am I thinking and feeling?' I discovered just how sad I was about leaving these many friends and fellow professionals with whom I had worked long and hard over eighteen years. Some sense of the enormous loss that I was about to experience swept over me. These friends would no longer be part of my daily life and I wouldn't be part of theirs. When the three Council speeches were finished I was invited to speak. I moved forward but only managed one or two words before I broke down in tears. I tried a couple of times to start again but it was hopeless. Suddenly I was overwhelmed by grief. I was acutely aware of the pain of parting but also the closeness and joy of present friendships. (Loader, 1997: 7)

From an emotional competences perspective, David Loader could be perceived as falling short on emotional self regulation and therefore in need of further emotional intelligence training. Indeed, he reports that many of his friends and colleagues discouraged him from disclosing this event in his book, therefore highlighting the taboo on emotional expression in professional circles. Yet as someone embarking on a chapter on self awareness in leadership I found myself immediately drawn to this man. I felt touched by his courage and willingness to show his vulnerability to his colleagues and subsequently to his readers. David Loader does not collude with his friends' protestations and includes the episode with some personal pride, conveying the alternative view that awareness of his emotions signals strength rather than weakness:

> The good news is that I was in this instance saved from myself so that I could experience the moment. I had been able to get in touch with my emotions on such an important occasion. (1997: 8)

Exercise

What were your emotional reactions to David Loader's account?

Where did you experience these in your body?

Is this a familiar or unfamiliar response on your part to emotionally charged public situations?

How easy would you find it to show your grief to colleagues?

How do you imagine they would receive and respond to your tears?

What do you think this says about you?

How can you account for your own reactions in terms of your personal experience
> – in your family?
> – in your working life?

Awareness: trusting self

Loader's story illustrates how being aware rests on and emanates from the capacity to be in touch with the inner world of sensation and feeling on a moment by moment basis. Awareness is characterised by immediacy and a willingness to acknowledge and heed the body's spontaneous responses to organismic needs (such as hunger, thirst) and environmental stimuli (such as, heat, cold, noise). It is this capacity to listen to and trust the internal process that builds self knowledge and self confidence. Leaders cannot expect people to trust them unless they have learned to value the wisdom of their own internal process and therefore trust themselves. Watkins describes self awareness as

> knowing what we feel in the moment and using that to guide our decision-making; having a realistic assessment of our own abilities and a well-grounded sense of self-confidence. (2000: 89)

There is an implicit assumption in the preparation for and execution of leadership functions that individuals must develop an understanding of leadership theories and skills to enable them to perform the range of tasks demanded of them. However, as Anna, head of an 'excellent' middle school said of her training for headship:

I learnt about task orientated strategic thinking which was useful but something else was missing to fit the real challenges of school leadership and improvement: preparation for the emotional onslaught that comes with it and how to self manage it. That I have learnt without specific training but by 'digging deep' whilst in the job as I imagine most headteachers do. Perhaps though we could do something better for the next generation of leaders. (M–H–I)

Anna and her school context may of course be an exceptional case. There is no intention on my part to impugn leadership development programmes. However, given that Anna's school moved from 'good' to a school judged by Ofsted as having 'many of the characteristics of an outstanding school' within two years of her appointment and Anna herself was designated an 'outstanding' leader by Ofsted within the same period of time, I was interested to find out what Anna felt had helped her achieve such success. Anna cited a number of factors, including the 'calibre of her staff and senior team, support from Governors and responsiveness by all to further developing a strong school ethos'. When asked to focus on her own contribution, her response reminded me of Evans' contention that 'outstanding leaders have inner sources of direction' (2000: 291). In the following extract, for example, Anna describes how developing self awareness helped her to find her own feet as a new head teacher:

I found myself thrown back on myself and having to really work out who I was and why I was struggling so much. I think I was still in shock. I hadn't considered how it would feel to sit in an office with my name and the word 'Headteacher' on the door and how heavily the responsibility would weigh on me.

Do you know what that was about?

Yes. I was the first and only member of my family ever to go to University, so to reach this point in my life just felt so momentous. Apart from the enormous sense of achievement and wanting to make a difference, I did feel self doubt creep in. The pressure was intense, you are constantly under scrutiny and have not earned the trust of colleagues – understandably that takes time.

That sounds challenging. Do you remember how you went about finding a way through your self doubt?

Well … it was like putting together a jigsaw … it wasn't quick or easy but eventually it all came together. I remember going to sleep at night and praying for answers … and answers did come, sometimes in my dreams and sometimes in the early hours when I woke up and lay there endlessly thinking about my life. Each memory was helpful but not enough on its own. I remembered stuff from being at school and from my family – I was one of eight kids in a family that had been through a lot of struggles – and from my years as a single mum, being a teacher and Head of Department and then a Deputy. I remembered things I had done well and things that people had said to me. I looked back over old cards and special stuff I had saved from kids, parents and colleagues. My husband, who had first put the idea into my head, was a great support. His belief in me meant a lot. He is in a leadership role in industry and wanted me to reach my full potential so I had a lot of support at home. All that was a real boost but it didn't stop me feeling inadequate on the inside. I was scared of failing the school and my family by not getting the balance of things right. It was a difficult point in my professional life but it was one I knew I could not give up on. It was a very painful point in my professional life.

So the final piece of the jigsaw … was?

It was when I thought about my own family background and kids … you see … I have three children of my own and three step children, and at the time three of them were going through middle school, so I thought about what I wanted for them and how important this stage in their lives is with adolescence and all the struggles many young people have to deal with, all that potential to be harnessed or lost and somehow, sounds silly I know … but I felt so full of love for them and pride in them and I knew I could bring that love to the job and give it to the pupils and to the staff and that I'd come out the other side. I just knew then that if I could hold onto that feeling and hold onto the expertise I had developed over the years, then I would be OK … and I have been. I try and take each day as it comes, prioritise actions, taking one step and action at a time and believe, hope and trust I can make it through. It is crucial to know how to resource that, to get the rewards from doing the job which can be great. (M–H–I)

Anna's story highlights the amount of self awareness and energy that is needed to move from followership to leadership. A certain amount of anxiety is normal and healthy when meeting personal challenges (Joyce, 1982) and helps to keep the leader focused and ready to learn from experience. Excessive anxiety and rumination, however, can be debilitating (Cox, 1978) and be exacerbated by feelings of isolation and loneliness associated with being 'at the top'. Leaders therefore need to balance finding support in their environment and finding support from within themselves to create an inner 'felt sense' of wholeness and competence. Paradoxically, it was Anna's patience and willingness to trust her inner world and to access personal support that led her to enhanced awareness and understanding of her personal jigsaw, thereby dispelling her paralysing self doubt. Anna's awareness and self knowledge effectively empowered her to recognise her own beneficence and her potential for effective leadership

What is awareness?

> Awareness is a form of experiencing. It is the process of being in a vigilant contact with the most important event in the individual/environment field, with full sensorimotor, emotional, cognitive and energetic support. (Yontef, 1979: 29)

Awareness is therefore a state of mind in which the individual is able to genuinely listen to the totality of their experience rather than to focus purely on the rational and intellectual. Being aware involves switching off one's usual state of consciousness to allow other faculties, such as feelings, intuition and creativity to be heard and therefore to avail the self of a greater range of information than normal. John Stevens (1971), a gestalt therapist and passionate advocate of awareness as a catalyst for personal growth, identifies three kinds of awareness, of:

- the outside world

- the inside world

- fantasy activity.

The first two are concerned with the immediate facts, the 'solid ground' of experience, and are therefore not subject to intellectualisation or rationalisation. Awareness of the outside world, for example, is concerned with present moment sensory experience, noticing the sounds, smells, taste, touch and images in the immediate environment. Awareness of the inside world is concerned with physical sensations inside the body, such as heat or cold, hunger or thirst, muscular tensions, aches and pains and manifestations of feelings. The third kind of awareness is concerned with unreality and focuses on the world of imagination. It includes:

> all mental activity beyond present awareness of ongoing experience: all explaining, imagining, interpreting, guessing, thinking, comparing, planning, remembering the past, anticipating the future. (Stevens, 1971: 6)

Fantasy activity therefore may inhibit awareness of the outside and inside world and lead the individual away from primary data. Equally, fantasy activity can help to process and make sense of primary data and aid the creative process of meaning making. Einstein, Beethoven and other renowned genii highlight the importance of relaxed awareness in moving into a different state of consciousness conducive to insight and creativity.

The following exercise is designed to help readers develop the three kinds of awareness identified by Stevens and can be fitted into a couple of minutes between meetings. If practised regularly it can not only help a busy leader learn to 'tune in' to themselves but also act as a quick centering exercise and aid relaxation.

Awareness 1

Create a two minute space in your day to discover something about your own awareness. Use this as a moment to focus in on yourself and give yourself some space from your routine. Close your eyes and focus on your breathing. Take a couple of deeper breaths. If possible, imagine yourself breathing in calm and relaxation with the in-breath and any stress or tension out with the out-breath. Let that go ... silently complete and repeat the same simple sentence stem several times:

Right now ... I am aware ...

Notice the focus and quality of your awareness and accept it without judgement ... let that go and taking a couple of deeper breaths return to the room and notice how you feel. Take a moment to reflect on the quality of your awareness and whether you focused more easily on the outside world, the inside world or on fantasy activity. Next time deliberately move away from this area and focus your awareness on the other two areas. Notice how that feels.

In the early stages of developing awareness, making space for such exercises involves a deliberate act, a commitment to explore the self-in-awareness. As with the development of any new way of engaging with self and the world, whether learning a teaching strategy or developing a posture to ease shoulder pain, there is likely to be some sense of unease and discomfort before the new becomes part and parcel of our repertoire of behaviour.

Two of the MEAZ primary schools had made concerted efforts to support the emotional development of pupils. In one of these, Sidegate School Lisa, the head teacher recognised soon after her appointment that the emotional climate of the school was a major contributor to pupil misbehaviour:

> When I was appointed here you could safely say that the school was in crisis. And that was due mainly to a management system that was based on bullying and on the head teacher not being able to manage the school effectively. There was no way of managing behaviour … and there was a blame culture where the head teacher blamed the teachers and the teachers blamed the children and the parents blamed everybody else. So it was a situation that was really out of control. The children were literally jumping in and out of the windows and I had to spend a lot of time on supporting the management on the children's behaviour first … because the teachers felt frightened, felt threatened in their own classrooms. So we got through that in the first two years. In the meantime we had an inspection, which took us into serious weaknesses, which was no surprise … (P–H–I)

Lisa's approach to the task of leading a school in crisis will be discussed in more detail later. Of relevance here is her recognition of the interrelatedness of pupil behaviour, emotional distress and learning and her determination to focus on all three simultaneously. She therefore heard the emotional distress of staff and pupils and, taking the emotional climate of the school very seriously, decided on a strategy of awareness raising:

> What I wanted to do was to open opportunities for children to learn how to learn … so that the children understood what they were learning, how they were learning and why they were learning … we felt that the children just weren't coming from language rich

environments and that we were at a great disadvantage ... they couldn't articulate their feelings or their thoughts so we gave priority to those areas. We decided to teach them how to be aware of their thoughts and feelings from nursery through to year 7. We have emotional check-in first thing each morning ... we introduced 'Thoughts and Feelings Books' for each child and gave each child their own lift-top desk so they have somewhere to keep them safe. We've used them in our key thinking skills. Just basically discussing different feelings and the words for them and discussing how they feel inside. We also do emotional focussing and they have to listen to their own voice and see their inner eye and lots of paired work. And they've been very, very expressive. We were really impressed by their use of language. It's made a big difference in many ways and really changed the way we see the kids ... it's the best thing ... stopped all the blaming and all the deficit talk ... the kids look forward to thoughts and feeling time too ... it's part of their routine now. (P–H–I)

Lisa's focus on meta-cognition and on emotional development is a key plank of her leadership strategy and has significantly contributed to pupil leadership and to the distribution of leadership functions amongst staff. This example lends support for the view that developing self awareness and self knowledge is a whole school issue and not just an issue for leadership or teacher development. For schools in extremely challenging circumstances it may come as some surprise that a focus on awareness can have such a powerful positive effect on pupil engagement with learning, pupil behaviour and on staff perceptions of pupils' capabilities. Lisa's school was awarded Beacon School status within three years of her appointment and she attributes some of this success to the development of an emotionally responsive teaching and learning strategy as well as a sustained focus on the school as a vibrant learning community.

Pupils at Sidegate school supported Lisa's contention that 'thoughts and feelings' books and time were an important part of their day. During my first group meeting with six pupils from years 5 and 6 I asked them what they liked about Sidegate school. I had specifically asked staff not to inform pupils of the reason for my visit and, at this point in the meeting, I had not mentioned the word feelings. I had told them I was interested in knowing more about their likes and dislikes about their school. They responded:

Rhys: I like everything about the school but I like the stuff, the work that we do best. I like how we do it with thoughts and feelings because I like sharing my feelings with other people.

Carrie: Yeah, we have a book and we write in it everyday in the morning when we come to school and we show it to the class and talk about it … it's about this big.
That sounds really good. How does that help you in school do you think?

Adam: I think it's good because you might be feeling sad or something and you're not sharing your feelings with no one and you write it in your book and you share it with the class and it makes you feel better in yourself because you learn how to share your feelings with someone. (P–P–FG)

Not surprisingly the pupils had a sophisticated and fluent grasp of emotional vocabulary as illustrated by some of the words they chose to describe the emotional content of their photographs:

Proud … excited … joyful … cheerful … comfortable … relaxed … impressed … sympathetic … disappointed … embarrassed … flabbergasted … mischievous

The pupils I interviewed (and they may of course not be a representative sample) demonstrated considerable care and thought about the issues in school that have an emotional impact on them and were able to use a wide-ranging emotional vocabulary to express their views. Their awareness of their own thoughts and feelings was supportive of the development of community amongst pupils and contributed to self esteem. These were important building blocks in the school's efforts to encourage and support authentic pupil leadership. A decision to give primacy to oracy (in advance of government directives) and to develop pupils' emotional narratives had enabled pupils to voice their needs and preferences and thereby to contribute to the school's change agenda. Members of the School Council had participated on residential weekends to develop their communication skills and their understanding of school democracy:

Carrie: We played like games so that we could get to know each other and activities where you had to speak out loud and argue for and against things so we get better at communicating and knowing how things happen.

It was the approachability of staff and their willingness to listen and support however, that pupils found most inspiring:

Chris: The teachers are understanding. They're always willing to help you in class.

Rhys: Yeh, and out of class too ... if we want something different they will listen.

Al: Like ... something what I'd like to have outside... all the boys that play football ... we wish that we'd get some new goalposts ... so we asked and Miss (head) said 'good idea' ... find out how much they are and think of some good ways of earning the money and we'll help you ... So we did that in maths and Miss X helped us, and then in English lessons we did our plan and made posters and we got nearly £100 already. (P–P–FG)

These pupils were definitely leaders in the making.

Awareness and creative problem solving

Awareness therefore can be learned, developed and fostered over time. It is also considered to be an essential part of creativity, 'a process typically born from frustration or the need for a solution' (Hecker and Kottler, 2002: 2). Indeed, frustrations *are often the thunderstorms guiding the lightning bolts of creativity'* (Kottler and Hecker, 2002: 8). Research into creativity highlights the futility of making strenuous efforts to find creative or innovative solutions to problems. Trying hard, it seems, inhibits the natural flow and rhythm of awareness and constitutes a kind of 'tuning out' from self rather than 'tuning in'. This view sits comfortably alongside Arnold Beisser's theory of the paradoxical nature of change. Beisser, a gestalt therapist, argues that

Change occurs when one becomes what he is, and not when he tries to become what he is not. Change does not take place through a coercive attempt by the individual or by another person to change him, but it does take place if one takes the time and effort to be what he is – to be fully invested in his current positions. (1970: 77)

When combined with acceptance of 'what is' and a non-judgemental view of one's awareness experience, the individual establishes a 'creative void', a space in which fresh insights can emerge into awareness. Kottler and Hecker (2002) identify four stages in the process of creative problem solving which resonate with Beisser's theory of human change and growth. *Preparation* and *incubation* involve creating space in which to tune into self and allow different levels of consciousness to emerge (relaxed awareness), *inspiration* is described as the moment of insight, and *verification* involves reviewing the insight and making sense of it in the light of existing knowledge. In this light it is possible to see Anna's 'inner work' of preparation for leadership as a creative endeavour and one which may have been important for her development as an outstanding leader.

In an interview with Howard Rosenthal (2002), Samuel Gladding identified creativity as a form of divergent thinking in which the 'a-ha' experience of insight is more likely to occur. He also identified developing the capacity to 'let things be' for a while as a crucial stage in the process. The process of incubation, he asserts, can be helped by drawing on the childlike spontaneity and freedom of play. Furthermore, he argues that people involved in the task of bringing out the creative abilities of others in a safe environment (such as teachers and leaders) have a duty to develop their own capacity for awareness, relaxation, persistence and playfulness. It is this experiential process that enables the leader to know what change and the creative process feels like on the inside and therefore to be more understanding, empathic and enabling of colleagues who are caught up in 'trying hard' to find solutions or to change aspects of their practice.

Anna describes how she practices awareness in the school day to support her problem solving. It is possible to discern clear similarities between the strategies she used to support herself during the first phase of her leadership and her ongoing work as a leader:

> At pressure points I just have to close my office for five minutes at regular intervals during the day and go inside myself. I need to do this to stop myself from imploding or exploding sometimes, at other times just to check out how I'm actually feeling. Otherwise the pressures are such that I could easily over-react or make a snappy and unwise decision that would cause me more problems later on.

Can you give me an example?

Well, this week has been full of frustration. One of the hardest things in the job is unreasonable demands by angry unreasonable parents. Also some feeling about the lack of local authority contact during Ofsted compared to the positive response since a really good report – this combined with the understandable demands of and interest in our new school build has all come at an already busy end of term. I've been really wound up about it so I have had to remove myself a couple of times this week just for a short while to sort myself out and decide how to handle the situation.

What do you do? How did you use that time?

Well, I ask my PA to only put emergency or urgent calls through for just a little while. I close my door which is normally always open. I check I have eaten first – I just cannot think straight when hungry! I focus on something and on my breathing. I usually have a problem to sort out, so I ask myself a question and notice what I'm feeling and let that help me get clearer about how I feel and what I need to do. Usually it does help and, if it doesn't help me find an answer on the spot it usually does later on when I'm not thinking about it. Anyway, what happens most of the time is that I feel calmer and a bit refreshed so it's not a waste of time. I know I should do it more often but it's hard to make that space during the school day. (M–H–I)

Anna deliberately interrupts her self-talk, comprised of thoughts, images and feelings, which interfere with the flow of immediate 'here and now' sensation. This ability to capture feeling states that can otherwise go unnoticed is essential for presence, where the individual is fully engaged in the moment and responding in a deeply connected and credible way. Senge et al.'s exploration of change in people, organisations and society led them to assert 'that the core capacity to access the field of the future is presence' (2005: 13). Presence, they argue, is essential for leadership of profound change.[1] It is about

'letting come', of consciously participating in a larger field for change. When this happens, the field shifts, and the forces shaping a situation can move from re-creating the past to manifesting or realising an emerging future. (2005: 14)

One of the key attributes of a leader's presence, as defined by Senge et al., is therefore founded on the dual processes of awareness and creative problem solving. In this state of incubation, or 'letting come', value is placed less on understanding and more on waking up to what 'is'. It is through this shift to direct awareness of what one is doing that one is able to recognise that other options are possible.

Awareness of needs

In humanistic psychology the value of awareness is its capacity to highlight and clarify personal needs and to help the individual identify personally (and socially) appropriate ways of ensuring these needs are fulfilled. Individuals are understood to be intrinsically motivated towards personal growth, to move through and beyond any rigid structuring of self towards a more flexible and response-able engagement with experience. This more fluid interaction of self with environment enables the individual to integrate thoughts, emotions and sensations and proactively develop their congruence, the 'fit' between their inner experience and their outer behaviour. Carl Rogers describes this pull towards growth as the actualising tendency:

> A directional trend which is evident in all organic and human life – the urge to expand, extend, develop and mature – the tendency to express and activate all the capacities of the organism, or the self. This tendency may become deeply buried under layer after layer of encrusted psychological defences. It may be hidden behind elaborate facades which deny its existence; it is my belief however, based on my experience, that it exists in every individual, and awaits only the proper conditions to be released and expressed. (1961: 351)

Developing awareness can therefore be understood as a key means to help individuals recognise the defences or façade they have constructed in order to survive their life experiences and to re-connect with their actualising tendency. In this way the individual can not only work towards meeting their immediate here and now needs (for space or shelter, for example) but also archaic needs that were unmet earlier in life and that led to the construction of their defences or façade. Awareness helps the individual to proactively work towards becoming authentic via greater self knowledge, self responsibility and self determination.

Even without awareness personal needs arise and clamour for attention until they are satisfied. Consider, for example, a baby that is hungry. The baby will cry until the caregiver works out what is wanted and responds with food. At that point the baby is satisfied, relaxes and falls off to sleep or lies gurgling in its cot. The baby follows what is variously called a cycle of awareness or cycle of experience from the moment of sensation until the moment of relaxed withdrawal into sleep or play. This cycle is instinctive and part of the natural expression of the life force and the human drive for growth.

From a humanistic perspective people have multiple needs and Maslow's (1943) hierarchy of needs is a helpful, if somewhat simplistic and mechanistic, representation of the gamut of human needs. In order to avoid being overwhelmed by a multiplicity of needs each person creates their own hierarchy which they manage moment by moment (for example drinking to relieve thirst before lying down to have a nap) or over a longer period of time (for example signing up to do a course in order to optimise chances of access to another course that will enhance career prospects).

If we return to Anna's account of her early days as a new head teacher then we can discern different order needs. On the surface we can understand Anna's situation as one of being overwhelmed by the demands of the job and the range of tasks she faced. This was the 'ground' of her experience. She talks of feeling paralysed, unable to find a way through. However, by paying attention to her experience and becoming aware of her anxiety, Anna's 'figural' (most pressing) needs were firstly to manage her anxiety, secondly to minimise her self doubt and thirdly, to believe in her potential as a leader. She drew on past experience, her dreams, her husband and some keepsakes to develop a felt sense of her competence and establish enough self belief to move forward. When responded to, the anxious figure receded creating space for the next need to emerge into figure and so on. This is part of the rhythmic pulsing of life and death, as 'figures' are formed and then dissipated. Anna's distress could also be understood within the 'ground' of her career development. Having wanted to move into headship for some time and having finally achieved her goal, Anna needed to work through her self doubt in order to fully feel her delight and pleasure in her success and embark wholeheartedly on her journey as a head teacher.

Perls et al. (1951) identified a number of stages on the cycle of experience between need or figure formation and dissipation and these are presented in Figure 4.1. It is important to note that sensation and awareness are fundamental to this process of figure formation and dissipation.

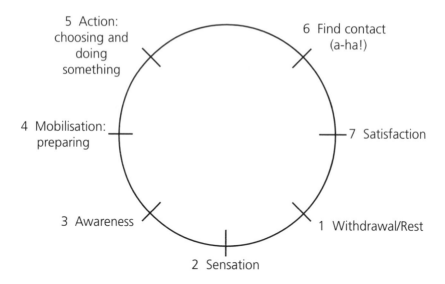

Figure 4.1: The Gestalt cycle of experience (adapted from Clarkson 2004)

If we use the example of Anna once more to understand these concepts in context, then we could speculate as follows. As Anna was familiarising herself with her new school and her new office and preparing to take up her role in the new academic year, (1) she found herself unable to concentrate. (2) She noticed a tenseness across her chest and shoulders, a shallowness to her breathing and butterflies in her stomach; (3) she became aware of feeling anxious and overwhelmed by her new role and responsibilities and (4) therefore created some space for herself over a number of days/weeks (5) to listen to her inner chatter, to her dreams, to memories of her school days, of university and of her different teaching roles and success as a deputy. (6) At the point of experiencing her love for her children Anna has a profound experience of felt connection with her own competence, an A-Ha moment, in which her anxiety dissolves and is replaced by a new sense of self knowing and (7) she is left with an inner glow of self knowledge and belief in her potential which sustains her through her headship. Anna's focus of attention is no longer preoccupied with concerns about her capabilities and she spends her time engaging with her life and the tasks of leadership until a new need emerges (1).

Awareness therefore serves several purposes. Firstly, it grounds the individual in the present moment and enables a deeper level of listening to self. This act of listening honours the self as a whole human being and helps to balance and counteract any negative effects arising from the shaking of society, community and education as well as the shaking involved in everyday school life. Thirdly, this awareness enables more creative ways of resolving problems in school and provides a model to help others develop their creativity and capacity for leadership. As Maslow said 'To be looking elsewhere for miracles is to me a sure sign of ignorance that everything is miraculous' (1971: 345). The leader's task is to bring out the miraculous in themselves and help others to do the same.

Exercise – the cycle of awareness

Take a small cycle (such as a physiological need, or buying an item of clothing for a special occasion, or going to the gym) and work your way around the cycle of experience. Start with either the withdrawal or sensation phase, whichever is easier … if possible, talk this through with another person and help them talk this through their own small cycle of experience. Use the following as a guide to help you:

1 Resting/relaxing
2 Noticing what is happening in your body
3 Becoming clear about the need
4 Summoning up the energy to do something
5 Doing it
6 Feeling the inner connection – the 'a-ha' moment when the need is met
7 Enjoying the feeling
1 Returning to rest/relax

Once you are comfortable with the concepts, repeat this process using a larger cycle (such as achieving a personal goal, your journey into leadership or 'coming out' in some aspect of your personal identity e.g. gender, sexual, racial, ethnic, physicality …).

Endnote

[1] In counselling and psychotherapy, the presence of the therapist is increasingly recognised as a key variable in developing trust and authenticity in the relationship between both parties and can go some way towards alleviating an inherent power imbalance.

5 *Understanding personal process*

Introduction

The Man is not a being but a bridge ... He has no being, he is a becoming. He goes on becoming, changing, moving from one point to another. He is a journey, a pilgrimage. (Osho, 1995)

Whilst many leaders and teacher leaders are driven by moral purpose and deep care for their students' growth and development, as people they have not always thought that deeply about their way of being and how this affects not only the quality of their relationships with students, colleagues and parents but also the quality of relationships that evolve between them. In this chapter we will explore how the cycle of awareness or experience can deepen awareness and understanding of habitual ways of being and acting and therefore develop one's capacity for authentic relationship and effective leadership.

If you develop the habit of engaging with your own cycle of awareness then you will begin to notice certain patterns, preferences or difficulties at different stages of the cycle. For example, you may find it difficult to tune into your sensations or to identify specific emotions. You may find that you tend to bypass the mobilisation stage and rush to do something without becoming clear about what it is you really need. You may find it is difficult for you to take pleasure in your achievement or to allow yourself some time to 'be' and 'let come'. Noticing and becoming aware of such patterns of self experiencing helps to develop an understanding of personal process, of personal ways of engaging with the self, with others and with the environment. An awareness of personal process is essential if leaders are to capitalise on their strengths and actively seek ways of balancing out or compensating for any personal weaknesses and limitations.

The process-oriented leader is profoundly aware of their own potential to influence for better or worse the creative process of meaning making for individuals and groups within the school community. They will therefore take full responsibility for their part in the field and for the impact of their behaviour on others. They make active choices about how they use themselves in the service of learning and human growth. At one end of the spectrum they might, for example, relate to the school and to staff as a bureaucrat, focusing first and foremost on balancing the budget, managing systems and quality assurance issues and keeping themselves out of meaningful relationship with the majority of the school community. At the other end of the spectrum they might choose to act as a nurturing parent, viewing their staff and students as people in need of their support, care and consistency and pay scant regard to systems and finances. Most leaders find their own way of being somewhere on the continuum between these two extremes.

Exercise

Where would you place yourself on the continuum between bureaucratic functions and people functions?

Systems   People/Relationships

I —————————————————— I —————————————————— I

Is that your choice or a state of affairs that has developed?

What is it about your personal process that has enabled this to happen?

A process-oriented leader is committed to self learning that is probing and honest enough to cope with the challenges presented within their own sphere of influence. This is essential work if they are to provide the conditions in which those they lead may work at a level that is both consistent with their capabilities and stretching and flexible enough to support creativity and leadership development. The self awareness and generosity of spirit that is required involves some intensive personal work on the part of the leader:

> First and foremost, this search for a more spacious self which can accommodate many perspectives has to be a personal quest, because we cannot presume to lead others to an expanded sense of identity if we are unable to embrace it ourselves. (Henzell-Thomas, 2004: 37)

This personal journey involves developing some clarity about personal patterns of relating to self and others and deepening the capacity for authentic personal experiencing and ways of being.

Authenticity is often cited as a key variable in perceptions of effective and well-respected leaders (Greenleaf, 1977; Sergiovanni, 1992; Evans, 1996). Authentic leaders are characterised by their trustworthiness, consistency, fairness, openness and moral character even when faced with the most challenging circumstances. Such qualities are constantly under scrutiny by others in the school environment and constantly under threat of erosion in the complex, busy morasse of school life and educational politics.

Authenticity is also strongly associated with trust in schools (Tschannen-Moran, 2004). However, authenticity is not a fixed state of being. Instead, it is a personal attribute which needs to be constantly attended to and nurtured. It is not easy to sustain the courage to lead and cope with all manner of negative and actively sabotaging responses from others. Authenticity develops from how one chooses to respond rather than from what one does and therefore involves no small degree of anxiety. However, few of the advocates of authenticity in educational leadership mention awareness as a key means of developing an authentic self.

In the following extract Shukla, a recently promoted change leader in an IQEA secondary school, describes how developing awareness of her own personal style, rhythm and pace has helped her to combat low self esteem, feel more confident in the senior leadership group in her school and give her a more authentic presence and voice:

> I have recognised that when I am in a group, I tend to sit back sometimes and listen … I sit quietly and I am very much aware that the others are uncomfortable about me because I am not taking part. But it is only because they may be saying things that I am not necessarily disagreeing with but I am trying to find ways of hearing what they are saying and becoming aware of how I feel about it before I say anything … some of the times when I do sit quiet is when [head] is saying something and I am thinking 'hang on, do I actually agree with this?'. That's when I go deep in thought and keep quiet … then I bring it back the week after at the next meeting … She is very sharp and I know if I say something without thinking that she will come back at me and I have not necessarily got that bit extra to give her … so I have to go away and really focus on my feelings and bring them to the fore … then I am confident to speak so it might not be that

meeting when I come out with something, it might be the next time
… It takes me time and I don't want to bully myself or agree to things
I don't believe in … what's the point in that? Maybe I've got something there about authority in the group. I have got to size things up
at first. It's also a way to look after myself. (S–TL–I)

Sam, head teacher of an infants school, similarly reports that by
enhancing her self awareness she has changed her relationship with
parents and found better ways of responding to their emotional distress:

By becoming more aware of myself and my own fears I have found
that I can … from when that angry parent comes through the door
… I can manage the situation so that I calm them down rather than
sending them through the roof and not going to the defensive
straight away. (I–HT–I)

Both Sam and Shukla focus awareness on their feelings as a guide to aid
their thinking and their behaviour.

The leader's way of being is the glue that makes their words and
actions either credible and trustworthy or suspect and anxiety-provoking
to those in their care and sphere of influence. Their power to make those
they lead feel tall or small cannot be over-emphasised. They can and do
make a significant difference to the lived experience of other members of
the school community. Therefore developing awareness of personal
process is a moral and ethical imperative for leaders wherever they are sit-
uated within the school environment, whether the kitchen, the school
office, the classroom, the playground or the head teacher's office.

Aspects of Personal Process

That our life is not consistent with the demands of society is not
because nature is at fault or we are at fault, but because society has
undergone a process that has moved it so far from healthy functioning, natural functioning, that our needs and the needs of
society and the needs of nature do not fit together anymore. Again
and again we come into such conflict until it becomes doubtful
whether a healthy and fully sane and honest person can exist in
our insane society. (Perls, 1970: 16)

Even the best intentioned and effective leader will find themselves
making their share of mistakes and misjudgements and be responsible for

causing distress to staff, parents, governors and pupils. They will equally find themselves being misjudged and misrepresented by staff, pupils and community and feel under attack from some quarter. This is inevitable as people work through their issues related to authority and power and foist the less trustworthy, fair, open and moral aspects of themselves onto the leader, therefore avoiding responsibility for these aspects of themselves. Just as communities, teachers and leaders have been systematically wounded and shamed by government control, scrutiny and mistrust, the resulting hurt, anger and distress can be intensified and perpetuated by further wounding and shaming of individuals and groups within the school and community environment (Blase and Blase, 2003).

In order to act morally and avoid getting caught in psychological traps set up to test trustworthiness, fairness and consistency, the leader will need an expanded awareness of self including their

* patterns of contact with self and environment

* vulnerable self: fears and anxieties.

They will also need awareness of their

* personal motivations for being an educator and leader

* personal culture and how this affects their way of being

* internal working model of leadership

* use of personal power.

All of these will play a significant part in the leader's relationship to self and will inevitably colour and shape interactions with others, playing a much greater role in the communication process than the particular words or phrases that are spoken.

Patterns of contact with self and environment

Rogers' (1961) concept of the 'actualising tendency' reflects a basic tenet of humanistic psychology, namely that the individual is basically healthy and striving for balance, health and growth. However, during childhood, the individual is dependent on their environment not only for shelter, food, warmth, love and so on but also for the development of their sense of self. The primary human need is for relationship and the emergent self of the baby is formed in the first instance via their physical sensations and their senses, through what they see, hear, taste, smell and so on, and how these are experienced as immediate feelings (Solms, 1996). The baby whose caregivers respond quickly, affectionately and accurately to meet a need for food, sleep or comfort will, over time, develop a more secure sense of self than one whose caregivers are too exhausted, depressed or 'high' to respond, and who therefore leave the baby to exhaust itself crying and fall to sleep without their basic needs being met.

Facilitative, attuned parents will do their best to respond to the child's unique disposition, rhythm and pace, whereas dysfunctional, unaware parents will respond to the child without due regard for their particular needs, treating them as a 'thing' that has to be fed and watered rather than nurtured. The baby's 'felt-sense' and emotional experience become part and parcel of self-experiencing. The baby with responsive, attuned caregivers will continue to express their needs and expect the environment to respond. They will experience consistent feelings of satisfaction and connection, whereas the baby with less aware and responsive caregivers will experience intense feelings of loss and abandonment.[1]

The baby and growing child that is only perceived to be acceptable or lovable if they do exactly as their parents or caregivers demand will therefore adapt their behaviour in order to maintain these significant relationships in a concerted effort to gain the love and approval they crave. This adaptation causes the child to deflect or abandon their organismic self and assume a false identity, or false self. Even the child with 'good enough' parenting (Winnicott, 1953), will normally have to give up some attributes of the real self (such as anger, or grief and their behavioural expression) in order to be acceptable within their own family or cultural environment. The cost to the individual of this process is the healthy flow of experience. No longer aware of their own intrinsic needs, the child's capacity to move easily and completely around the cycle of experience, and therefore to develop fully into a mature, emotionally healthy adult is impaired.

Exercise

Close your eyes and, in your imagination, create a black and white cine-film of your childhood. Just observe, as if a witness to this young life. What title would best fit the story unfolding in front of you? Notice how you feel ...

Are you aware of any aspects of yourself that you had to 'give up' in order to survive and thrive in your family home?

It often takes a life changing event, such as the break up of a marriage, loss of a job or death of a close relative to alert the individual to any discrepancy between the presenting self and the raw data of real (and confusing) feelings. Many individuals seek support through counselling or psychotherapy in order to manage a particular problem and are surprised to find that they are grieving for more than their marriage, their job or a relative. Developing awareness of their sensations and feelings can help to rediscover a grieving or lonely child within who is longing to be seen, heard, loved and accepted just as they are.

Perls (1969) and Perls et al. (1951) considered interruptions to the healthy cycle of experience as a major cause of dis-ease because the flow of energy around the cycle is interrupted or blocked, therefore leaving the need unfulfilled and the individual dissatisfied.

> When people do not move easily and spontaneously around the awareness cycle to get their needs met, the event is unfinished. Some episode of childhood history, some important early need, was left unsatisfied and the person did not complete the cycle in a way that was right for him or her biologically or psychologically. For example, a child not being allowed to grieve (or cry) for the death of a beloved pet may lead the grown-up person to withhold affection from new attachments since the original grief was not allowed its full expression in a way that was healthful/harmonious for animals and human beings. (Clarkson, 2004: 51)

This example illustrates how 'unfinished business' can affect the capacity for emotional expression, connection or satisfaction in later relationships. In a society in which the expression of emotions is still taboo, children and young people are often chastised by angry caregivers for expressing their pain, sadness, anger, resentment and jealousy. If these emotional expressions are consistently interrupted and disapproved of, then the child will learn to interrupt sensation and awareness and thereby disavow particular emotions and ban them from awareness.

Exercise

In your family of origin how acceptable was it for *you* to express:

Anger Anxiety Disappointment Fear Frustration Guilt Hurt Impatience Irritation Jealousy Pain Revulsion Sadness?

Compassion Curiosity Pleasure Interest Tenderness Empathy Joy Love Satisfaction Passion?

Incomplete experiences and feelings persist in the memory while the actualising tendency seeks ways of concluding any situation or interaction that is unfinished:

> These incomplete directions do seek completion and when they get powerful enough, the individual is beset with preoccupation, compulsive behaviour, wariness, oppressive energy and much self-defeating behaviour. (Polster and Polster, 1973: 36)

Unfinished business can manifest in many ways such as depression, or a victim mentality in which the individual feels misunderstood and mistreated even when those around them are doing their utmost to support them. Perls (1969) perceived it as a way of avoiding facing difficult or painful feelings from the past. Eric Berne (1967) describes this as a 'poor little me' game, which serves to avoid taking responsibility for one's own behaviour and therefore making meaningful contact in the present.

It is inevitable that everyone has some unfinished business from the past that inhibits motivation and capacity for engagement in the present. Much of the time this does not directly interfere with day to day functioning. However, at times of personal challenge or organisational change an individual's unfinished business can become mobilised and work to sabotage the self and the organisation. A rational desire to change and grow can be severely challenged by the need for emotional safety, consistency and predictability which fuel active and passive methods of resistance. However, as Anna says 'when the foes come and get you, which they inevitably do, you must be able to ride above it' (M–H–I).

Without awareness of personally unresolved issues a leader may also find themselves emotionally caught up in someone else's 'game' or interpersonal rivalry with personally damaging results.

Exercise

Reflect back on the previous exercise.

Focus on those feelings that were unacceptable in your family of origin.

Select one to focus on for the next four or five minutes.

Can you recall any specific incident or series of incidents in your family that made you aware that this was unacceptable?

As you remember be aware of any sensations in your body and stay with them …

Notice any residual feelings about the event(s).

Is there any 'unfinished business'?

If so, how might this affect your leadership?

Impediments to awareness

According to Perls et al. (1951) there are four key ways of interrupting the cycle of experience, namely introjection, projection, retroflection and confluence. Later Polster and Polster (1973) added deflection.

Introjection

Introjection is the unquestioning acceptance and internalisation of the attitudes and ideas of significant others. Introjectors act as they believe others want them to act and thereby curb any awareness of their own 'truth'. It is of course important that children and young people introject cultural messages and know how to behave appropriately in social situations. However, introjection can also be used by a child to avoid conflict with caregivers and significant others. Perls used the term 'shouldism' to reflect this process whereby social and religious taboos, the persistent disapproval or contempt of others and dissatisfaction with a person's behaviour or performance, are accepted as true, internalised and turned against the self, resulting in a form of intrapersonal bullying. This internal dialogue is literally dominated by the 'should' word and includes messages, such as:

* You are fat – you *should* go on a diet.

* You *shouldn't* be so lazy/selfish.

* You *should* have completed that scheme of work by now.

* You *shouldn't* be so slow/fast; loud/quiet; stupid/clever.

It is as if there is an internal splitting process at work, which Perls et al. (1951) describes as the topdog–underdog polarity. The topdog is authoritarian, harsh and judgemental, while the underdog is apologetic and submissive. The task for the individual is to integrate these two polarities of self into a more balanced relationship in which neither dominates and the individual can stop being at war with themselves.

Perls maintains that 'shouldism' in adults reflects a childlike desire to please others rather than to respond to ones' own genuine (organismic) needs. Lisa, head of a primary school offers a potent example of 'shouldism' at work when she talks about her desire to please the local authority more than to follow her own values:

I made a big mistake last year and I was very irritated because the year before we got very good SATS results and so therefore, even though we knew the cohort was not as strong, we set equally ambitious SATS results and we didn't get them. And the morale of the staff just hit rock bottom … that was very foolish of me … I paid too much attention to something that makes us look good out there rather than what is good about what we do … There is a part of me that wants to prove something to authority and when I get caught in that, that's when I make mistakes and make myself, the staff and the pupils suffer. That sounds awful I know, but I like to think I have learned from that. (P–H–I)

Lisa's willingness to own her grandiosity and her need for recognition and approval helps her to recognise her internal bully in action. Lisa is aware that there are different aspects to her personality and recognises that her behaviour has had negative repercussions for her staff. She therefore demonstrates awareness of a more compassionate, responsible and secure sense of self. Lisa's awareness of her process and of different aspects of herself enable her to question her introjects and to mobilise her own energy to rectify the situation. Introjection interrupts the mobilisation/action phase of the cycle of experience.

Projection

Clarkson describes projection as 'seeing in others what I don't want to acknowledge in myself' (2004: 62). In projection individuals do not accept their own feelings, limitations or vulnerabilities. Instead, they deny them and foist them onto another who is then often made responsible for directing the feelings/attitudes back onto the projector. Prejudice, for example, is a particular form of projection in which disowned attributes of the oppressor, such as laziness, sexual depravity, stupidity, greed and so on are attributed to the oppressed group, thereby relieving the projector of responsibility for these aspects of their own personality. Leaders are often subject to projections from staff, pupils and community, who prefer to blame them than take responsibility for their own behaviour or lack of support for policies or procedures designed to effect change. They may accuse the leader of ignoring them while being unaware (and often unwilling to become aware) that it is they who are ignoring the leader. Individuals project those aspects of their behaviour which are at odds with their introjects, so that they can play victim and transfer their aggression onto others. Some young people are highly adept at this, blaming the teacher for their failure, instead of recognising that they have failed to complete their homework or to do any adequate revision themselves. Projection therefore interrupts the action phase of the cycle of experience.

Retroflection

Retroflection is the act of doing to self what one wants to do to others, or others to do to them. Instead of being angry with parents for example, some young people turn their anger in on themselves and self-harm. Instead of asking for support or comfort many people turn to food to comfort themselves. Retroflection is commonplace in class-rooms and schools where young people and adults alike do not trust the environment to meet their needs.

> People may learn to retroflect when their feelings and thoughts are not validated in their families of origin or when they are punished for the expression of their natural impulses. The impulse to hit out remains locked in the person's body, affecting muscular patterns, abdominal tension and chemical imbalances in the body. Energy is used to suppress the original held back impulses, thereby also draining energy away from the person's capabilities of his or her needs met in the current environment. (Clarkson 2004: 63)

Retroflection in other words involves some form of self-harm or emotional holding 'in', which needs to be expressed in more constructive ways. Schools therefore need to provide safe spaces for adults and for young people to talk through their problems and learn to receive support from their environment (Renwick and Spalding, 2002). Stress can be and suicide is an extreme form of retroflection. Similarly, narcissism is a form of retroflection as narcissists do not trust the evaluations of others and rely heavily on their own (often excessive) self-valuing. Retroflection can occur at any phase of the cycle but is most often associated with the final contact (or 'a-ha') phase as individuals interrupt their capacity to fully connect with their feelings.

Confluence

Confluent individuals blur the boundary between themselves and their environment. They cannot tolerate difference and will therefore feel most at home with people with whom they experience a sense of merger or oneness and a loss of their own identity. Confluent individuals prefer the use of 'We' rather than 'I' and lose all sense of their own identity and needs. The merger with another may be to do with beliefs, attitudes or feelings. Physical separation is experienced as a threat and the unwritten rule between confluent individuals is 'We agree not to disagree'. The use of the word 'We' is indicative of this interruption to the cycle. How can a person develop awareness if they do not see themselves as a separate unity and if being an individual or separate is actively resisted?

Confluent people resist change because it threatens to change the relationship between self and the environment:

> Confluent people see to it that nothing new happens; yet at the same time little that is interesting or exciting happens in their relationship. (Harman, 1982: 47)

Some confluence in the workplace is necessary and healthy. The identification of the individual with their role or with their school can be a great source of loving energy. However, leaders and teachers need to be aware of their desire for unhealthy confluence, for others to think or act in the same way as they do. This is particularly acute in organisations where leaders' intimate partners or closest friends are also professional colleagues and where there is a high degree of reliance on one another for support. Unless dissent is valued as necessary and healthy within the school some pairings may collude to label certain individuals as difficult or obstructive and fail to hear or engage with different and potentially important perspectives. Such self deception limits the capacity for co-creating an inclusive school and, fed up of being neither heard nor respected, demoralised individuals eventually find ways of coping that keep themselves safe but leave valuable resources and energies untapped.

It is therefore imperative that leaders are aware of their capacity to tolerate differences in belief, behaviour and attitudes. Effective leadership involves a willingness to engage in debate, take risks and experiment with new behaviours and new ways of being. By contrast, management focuses on maintaining the status quo whilst tinkering with language and presentation to impress those on the outside that important changes are in process.

Deflection

This interruption involves reducing one's awareness of the environment in order to avoid pain or distress to self. In actively avoiding awareness of self and environment the individual is left without quality of contact with another and can therefore feel missed or abandoned, which is probably a repetition of their early life experience and therefore a familiar feeling in social situations. Equally, their awareness of the environment lacks colour, texture or depth and therefore dilutes the quality of their experience. Such individuals bring little energy to their contact with the environment and will tend to avoid highly charged and passionate situations, reducing them to rational scrutiny and judgement. Many children deflect from feeling in school as a way of avoiding being picked on, humiliated or shown up. Teachers too may deflect from awareness of their own behaviour and how this might be contributing to problems in their classroom or their team.

In addition Perls identified another way of engaging with self and the field which he perceived as inhibiting the process of self knowing. This he called 'aboutism'.

Aboutism

Aboutism is found in intellectualisation and rationalisation, which Perls describes as placing distance between self and experience. This, he claims, is established by taking up a superior, often critical stance towards self and others and to alternative ways of seeing. Aboutism

> lets us talk about things, gossip about ourselves or others, broadcast about what's going on in ourselves, talk about our cases. Talking about things, or ourselves and others as though we were things, keeps out any emotional responses or other genuine involvement.
> (Perls, 1970: 15)

In the current educational climate aboutism is a prevalent and effective method of protecting the self from the full emotional impact of field conditions, such as successive educational reforms or difficult classroom situations. It is also a valuable strategy to keep an inquiring researcher of the emotional climate in school at bay! The tape transcripts reveal some reluctance on the part of teachers and head teachers to express their own emotional experience within the school environment. This is not surprising in a culture in which emotions and the expression of emotions is still largely taboo. Talking 'about' colleagues, pupils or parents is not only more prevalent but also safer and less exposing.

Exercise

If you reflect on the past 24 hours of your life, can you identify:
- ways in which you have deflected from attending to your sensations and your feelings?
- how introjected messages or 'shoulds' from childhood have affected your capacity to respond effectively to a situation?
- anyone you have had strong feelings towards? Is it possible that you have projected a feeling or an (in)competence onto them, or they onto you? Be honest!
- anyone at school who you seek out in order to share a concern and who you know will agree with you and support you?
- ways in which you turn any of your needs back on yourself or retroflect? Do you, for example:
  - eat chocolate, biscuits or crisps when you are not hungry?
  - starve yourself when you are hungry?
  - drink too much coffee/tea?
  - smoke?
  - drink too much alcohol?
  - take recreational drugs?
  - drive too fast?
  - abuse your body – for example, over or under exercising?

Becoming aware of the way in which a leader interrupts the quality of their awareness and of the natural rhythm of gestalt formation and dissipation is an important step on the journey towards wholeness and authenticity. As awareness of learned habits and blocks to awareness increases, so does the capacity to make choices and experiment with new behaviour. Changing habitual patterns of engaging with, avoiding or distorting experience is no easy process if this becomes a personal battleground and means for warring with the self. However the leader, who can accept and value their own process as part of the younger self's 'creative adjustment' to a particular set of environmental and field conditions, is more likely to experience a subtle, gradual loosening of rigid, fixed ways of engaging with self. 'Tuning into' self allows the more vulnerable and disowned aspects of self to be known and appreciated as valuable sources of information. Appropriate humility helps to protect the leader from a gradual slide into arrogant and grandiose ways of being and to sustain the capacity for empathy that is central to the emotional work of teachers and leaders. The following chapter will explore the significance of awareness of the leader's vulnerable and shadow self within the context of wounding, and wounded, leadership.

Endnote

[1] There is growing evidence from neuroscience that the brain development of babies who suffer emotional neglect and/or abuse is significantly impaired. The areas of the brain that fail to develop healthily are those associated with emotional development. For more detailed information see Gerhardt (2004) and Shore (1994).

6   *Wounding self and others*

Introduction

Catherine had worked at Meadow High School for 15 years, having returned to teaching after a six year break to bring up her young children. Popular with staff and students due to her optimistic disposition, incisive sense of humour and creative mind, Catherine's attention to detail and reliability made her an excellent administrator. Not surprisingly, therefore, Catherine was encouraged to apply for management and leadership positions within the school and was appointed as assistant principal following the arrival of a new and dynamic head teacher, Duncan.

Duncan was keen to bring new blood into the senior management team and to change the school culture from authoritarianism and control to collaboration and shared responsibility. Catherine's friendliness, energy and reputation as a hard worker impressed him and it was not long before he trusted her with the day-to-day operational running of the school. Meanwhile, he took charge of the school plan and began to restructure the organisation to meet the demands of workforce remodelling and The Children Act 2004. He met every member of staff to get to know them, assess their potential for leadership and identify the 'best fit' between individual strengths and strategic roles across the school community. Despite some resistance from longer serving colleagues, Duncan successfully involved and motivated staff to keep an open mind about the change process and to develop the skills necessary to implement change effectively. He found the whole process both exhilarating and exhausting.

At the end of each school day he would spend up to an hour with Catherine to debrief the day and plan for the next one. He found her easy to talk to and gradually disclosed more of his anxieties with her, particularly about his handling of difficult or sensitive issues. Catherine was usually helpful and insightful and he became quite dependent on her regular support and advice, for which he was always grateful.

Catherine however, felt put upon and, unwilling to discuss this with Duncan in case it affected her performance-related pay, began to discuss with other senior staff some of the 'emotional demands' he made of her. Their judgement of Duncan began to change as they too noticed more of his limitations, particularly his lack of attention to detail and his dependency on Catherine for information and advice.

The situation became more intense when the local authority (LA), who were impressed by the school's transformation and enhanced pupil achievement, asked him to represent the school or LA at conferences and leadership training events, and also called on him to mentor other struggling head teachers. Slowly, other staff became aware that all was not well in the senior management team. Somehow, all the positive energy, experience and creativity Duncan had brought to the school was outweighed by negative gossip. The head found himself increasingly isolated and Catherine, whilst still apparently supporting him in private, challenged him robustly at every opportunity in senior team meetings. Duncan initially welcomed the challenges. It took him a little while to realise that his relationship with Catherine was not as he had thought. He began to question her loyalty and soon realised his trust in her had been misguided. When he challenged her she retaliated telling him that he was more interested in his own career than in the school.

Shocked by this revelation, Duncan began to make sense of the different responses he had received from staff and governors during his third year in office and to understand that Catherine's support and advice had come at a price. Catherine became more openly adversarial and cynical and won the chair of governors over to the view that Duncan was not really 'man enough' for the job and had used staff and school to further his own career. A distraught and disbelieving Duncan took advice from the National Association of Head Teachers (NAHT) who felt he had grounds for complaint. However, he also realised that in taking this action he would merely affirm and collude with Catherine's claims. He therefore chose to put the best interests of the school before his own and negotiated a new post with the LA to leave staff free to focus their energy on teaching, learning and pupils rather than on conflict in the leadership team. He continued to use his experience and skills in leadership to support other head teachers and schools but never set foot in Meadow High again.

After his departure the governors asked Catherine to stand in as acting head. Despite advertising the post three times they were, however, unable to appoint. Rather than perpetuate any distress caused by the conflict and lack of a permanent head teacher, the governors offered Catherine a five year contract as head teacher. Catherine was keen to make a good impression on the governors and LA and to prove herself competent enough for the task. She therefore responded affirmatively to all demands from the LA and the school became involved in numerous new initiatives. When staff began to complain that these new initiatives involved far too much work, Catherine justified her position by comparing Meadow High with other schools. There was an underlying assumption on Catherine's part that staff were lucky to work at such a good school with such able pupils and supportive governors and parents. When people began to question some of her decisions she dismissed their concerns and blamed pastoral and curriculum leaders for not implementing initiatives effectively. Some staff began to feel demoralised and defeated by her refusal to take their feedback seriously. Unusually, a number of staff including two middle leaders went off sick with stress-related illness over the first two years of Catherine's leadership. Many more complained of feeling overburdened. Catherine viewed these staff as 'difficult' and 'inadequate' and expressed the view that 'They don't know the half of it'. At the end of her term of office Catherine's contract was renewed. The governors were impressed by her presentation of the school's successes. Staff, however, did not feel that her account reflected reality. Many were horrified that Catherine's desire to be perceived as successful had made her deaf and blind to their experience. They called her the 'Iron Woman' and several of them had begun to question the events that had precipitated Duncan's departure from the school.

Catherine's energy, efficiency and ambition are key motivators on her journey into leadership. Her excellent human relations skills enable her to make good quality contact with staff and help them to trust her judgement. Unfortunately however, Catherine has paid a huge personal price for her success – she has lost her humility and with it her capacity for empathy.

Catherine's focus on doing and achieving and her need to prove herself by working harder than any of her staff has caused her to neglect her more vulnerable side and to keep her insecurities, fears and anxieties submerged so that they do not interfere with her ambition. Similarly, she has kept the less socially acceptable aspects of her personality hidden from view so that no-one in school experiences the force of her anger, envy or contempt directly, although most people are aware of feeling subtly controlled and put down in her presence. Catherine is proud of her capacity for self regulation and unaware of how her negative feelings seep into her contact with others.

When Duncan begins to lean on Catherine for support and to disclose his insecurities, Catherine's efforts to block awareness of her own vulnerabilities have to be intensified. Duncan challenges Catherine's internal working model of what it means to be a leader. From her perspective, a leader and a real professional is someone who is rational at all times, self sufficient and does not lean on anyone for support. The maintenance of this belief has consequences for Catherine's capacity to empathise with others. If Catherine does not complain about her workload, then why should others complain about theirs? If she does not waste time feeling sorry for herself, why should others? If she manages her emotions, why should others voice feelings of inadequacy or fear and want a response? Such thoughts make Catherine angry and resentful and, unable to contain both her vulnerability and her anger, her resentment 'leaks', firstly towards Duncan and then later towards those staff who feel overloaded and stressed. Her contempt and gossiping combine to force Duncan into an impossible situation. Fortunately, his integrity enables him to make a principled decision about his position in the school and to simultaneously take care of himself.

In the meantime Catherine becomes more disconnected from herself and from her colleagues. She compensates by relying on her family for support and developing an inner caucus of staff who are confluent with her. A good line in rhetoric helps her to impress and convince outsiders about her competence and to sustain a self-image in which her version of reality is superior to any other. In order to really develop the school community, however, Catherine needs to revisit her internal working model of leadership, reconnect with her values and embrace the less acceptable aspects of herself. In this way she will find less destructive ways of taking care of herself and managing the emotional demands of her role.

Beatty (2000) highlights the paradox that competent but emotionally unaware leaders such as Catherine contribute to their own demise when they inflict emotional wounds on others. Leaders therefore have an ethical and moral duty of care to develop their capacity for real emotional connection:

> Schools run on love – of the kids, the subject, the work, the hope, the possibilities, the smiles of satisfaction, the looks of appreciation, the little things that keep teachers and students and leaders

going. The principal whose interactions with staff undermine this all-important source of energy by creating dissociation between teacher's self-confidence and their professional self-image is like the captain drilling a hole in her/his own ship. No matter how hard you bail, it's always sinking. Leaders who cause teachers emotional damage would be wise to reconsider the cost-effectiveness, if nothing else, of disintegrating a teacher's self, a precariously balanced entity that is already overtaxed. (Beatty, 2000: 336)

Given a number of high-profile court cases against bullying and harassment in the workplace (Barkham, 2006) and the prevalence of teacher harassment by school leaders (Blase & Blase, 2003), Beatty sends a warning shot across the bows of school leadership. The education system can ill afford high profile costly settlements that serve to reinforce negative public perceptions of teachers and schools.

There is little doubt that leaders have the power to evoke strong emotions in those they lead. As Munby says:

We can't easily talk ourselves out of a situation we have behaved ourselves into. They will forget what we say but they will never forget how we made them feel. Relationships matter. (2006)

However, as we have already seen in the previous chapter, leaders may also have a precariously balanced sense of self. The presumption that 'toxic leaders' (Lipman-Blumen, 2005)[1] are solely or chiefly responsible for mistreatment in schools is misleading. In reality, many leaders such as Duncan are also the victims of emotional wounding by staff, parents, governors or LA.

Sarah, head of a primary school, described the early phase of her leadership as an 'assault course'. Sarah had taken over the headship from Helen, a matriarch, who had run the school with benign intent for more than 25 years and resisted all efforts by the LA to influence the culture of the school and enhance the quality of teaching and learning. Helen and her staff were committed to the pupils' well being. The school environment was safe and happy and Ofsted had judged the school to be 'satisfactory' in most areas. Helen and her staff believed this was 'as good as it gets' given the location of the school on a highly impoverished council estate. Nothing could dissuade Helen from this deficit view of pupils and parents. The relationship between herself and the LA School Improvement Team disintegrated to the point where

Helen decided to take early retirement at very short notice, much to the distress of her staff. Sarah's arrival at the start of the following term was greeted with much mistrust and staff viewed her as implicit in the LA's 'despicable treatment' of Helen. In the first year of her headship Sarah experienced a series of personal attacks from staff as they vented their anger, resentment and judgement towards the LA on her. Sarah felt 'persecuted' and 'sabotaged' in all she said and did:

> I felt as if I was being hunted by a pack of animals. No matter how hard I tried they misread and misheard everything I did and said. Every comment started with 'when Helen was here we …'. I decided the only way forward was to roll my sleeves up and prove these kids could do more than they gave them credit for, to lead by example … so when a member of staff went off sick I took over her class. That was when I started to regain some equilibrium.

What do you put that down to?

Developing good relationships with the children and their parents kept me sane and the deputy head supported me. She got ostracised because of that. It was terrible … parents were treated like kids by teachers and admin staff.

Can you give me an example?

The office staff were in the habit of making parents and pupils wait even when they did have time to speak to them. The kids were managed and controlled … patronised really … and not stimulated and engaged in meaningful learning. I felt I had no choice but to lay down the law about what was and was not acceptable behaviour … fortunately I had good support from the LA but it was soul destroying work and when I look back I don't really know how I survived. Several of the staff voted with their feet, which was sad and I felt I had failed as a head. They objected to everything: to staff development events on teaching and learning; to the introduction of circle time; to training parents as classroom helpers … it was only when I appointed new staff from elsewhere that things began to change and I stopped feeling like a lone voice in the wilderness. (P–H–I)

Sarah's story highlights how new leaders can become caught up in the web of historical power relationships and feel victimised by staff who have no other legitimate outlet for their frustration and anger whether about the past or about change itself. Becoming aware of emotional processes which inhibit the work of teams and schools, such as dependency, anger (fight) and abandonment (flight) can help the leader to steer a steady course and resist the temptation to get enmeshed in a dramatic role (such as persecutor, victim, rescuer), which only serves to intensify rather than de-fuse the situation.

Exercise

Take a few minutes to tune into yourself and to reflect on your membership of a group or team in school ... How did you feel being in this team? How did you feel about the team leader? How did your feelings affect the way you behaved in the group?
In what ways did you support the work of the leader and group?
In what ways did you undermine or sabotage the work of the leader and group?
Take a moment to reflect on these words and see how they fit with your experience:

Optimistic	Cynical	Dominating	Passive
Generous	Supportive	Caring	Involved
Sharing	Holding back	Avoiding	Encouraging
Challenging	Gossiping	Colluding	Pretending

Leaders are human beings first and foremost and therefore have their own fair share of fear and anxieties, whether related to self doubt or being judged negatively by others. Their vulnerability, however, is rarely considered or acknowledged within the school community as people either dehumanise and denigrate leaders (as in Sarah's case) or invest them with super human powers. Both processes are fundamentally unhealthy for the individual and for the school:

> Many of us want leaders who project an aura of certainty – real or imagined – that we lack within ourselves. If the leaders are not actually knowledgeable and in control, to satisfy our own desperate needs, we convince ourselves that they truly are. In the process, we occasionally push leaders into believing in their own omniscience. Some, of course, don't need much of a push. (Lipman-Blumen, 2005: 32)

Catherine certainly believed in her own sense of omniscience and needs a push into humility to stem the ebbing morale of staff before it negatively affects the quality of teaching and learning and the student experience. This chapter explores the themes identified through Catherine and Duncan's story in more depth, starting with the concept of the leader's vulnerable self.

The Vulnerable Self

> Those who are certain of the good that they do are more to be feared than those who are more willing to admit and struggle with their own personal limitations, to share their doubts and to express their values. (Fagan, 1970: 103)

Leadership is an inherently ethical endeavour (Block, 1993), a 'moral art' (Hodgkinson, 1991: 27). Ethical leadership in schools is rooted in human integrity, in being responsive and reflective in the face of complex problems. A leader's capacity to acknowledge their human vulnerability is one essential ethical safeguard to prevent them from hiding behind or abusing their status and power.

For many leaders feeling vulnerable is an everyday occurrence. In her book *The Achilles Syndrome*, Petruschka Clarkson describes her experiences of working as a therapist with high achievers and leaders who experience a mismatch between their abilities and their confidence and whose lives are therefore dogged by secret fear of failure:

> Their sense of competence feels as if it is built on sand, always subject to threat, to exposure, to shame, and to public humiliation. When the performance is over, there is only the relief that 'This time I've not been found out. What a lucky break – I've been able to hide the shortfall between what people have come to expect of me and what I actually feel I can deliver'. ... (Clarkson, 1994: 6)

Of course, many leaders do not experience excessive anxiety in anticipation of a new task, or exhaustion and relief on its completion and an inability to carry over any sense of achievement to the next task, all of which are characteristics of the Achilles Syndrome. One of the questions on the SWOT analysis of the emotional audit asked teachers and leaders to write about aspects of their role that prevent them sleeping at night or that wake them in the early hours. The majority of them described people problems, such as dealing with angry parents, underperforming teachers or vulnerable children at risk of exclusion. A second category involved practical matters, such as organising work experience, dealing with excessive paperwork and supervising a new school build.

It is highly likely that concerns about competence, accuracy of judgement and fear of failure underlie these presenting problems. However, given the prevailing climate and the collective sense of vulnerability in the teaching profession (Bullough et al., 2006) it is not surprising that respondents declined from disclosing such vulnerable aspects of self, particularly in writing.

It is important to recognise that the development of a false self and the interruptions to awareness and experience discussed in the previous chapter can be understood as a healthy survival mechanism and a creative adjustment to the field conditions in childhood. The resulting self-talk and patterns of behaviour are, however, often inappropriate for adulthood and not easily amenable to change, as is evident in Catherine's case. Attention needs to be paid to the vulnerable, hurt self that has been neglected and may have been kept out of awareness by the original adaptation. Eleanor Roosevelt believed fear to be important for leadership development in that it reminds the leader of the fragility of life and re-connects them with their core values and their organismic self:

> You gain strength, courage, and confidence by every experience in which you really stop to look fear in the face. (Roosevelt cited in Lipman-Blumen, 2005)

The Johari window (Luft, 1984) is helpful in drawing attention to the hidden self in the context of self-disclosure (Figure 6.1). The secret self contains those aspects of self that are kept hidden from everyone except perhaps those with whom the individual is most intimate. It is the contents of the secret self that make individuals feel vulnerable, either because they are precious and treasured or because they are sources of hurt and shame and therefore make the individual fear exposure, ridicule or humiliation.

The vulnerable self can, however, become hostage to the internal bully, the topdog–underdog dynamic described earlier, and therefore perpetuate feelings of inferiority, anxiety or terror from childhood days. It is only in attending to this vulnerable self and in valuing its role in keeping the child safe that healing can occur. Indeed Carl Rogers (Baldwin, 2000) insists that the capacity to help another depends on the ability to recognise, accept and own one's vulnerabilities. In doing so a leader stops wasting energy defending themselves. Equally, it is only when the leader is in touch with their own imperfections, flaws and anxieties and able to accept them as a valuable source of knowledge and creativity, rather than as an enemy, that they will be able to offer appropriate support and care to those most vulnerable within the school community. Otherwise, others may 'pick up' on the leader's vulnerability and find it confusing as well as distancing. In one school, staff described their head as 'an enigma' and described how they would not go to her if they felt distressed. There was a consensus amongst staff that she might listen but be unable to hear them:

> I think she would [listen], but she wouldn't want to really take it on board, because she'd either go in tears herself, and I'd think 'oh, god, now I've upset her', or, I don't know, I don't understand her. She's either quite tearful, or almost distant, and I really can't make her out. But she's certainly nobody that I would share things with. (J–TL–FG)

It is impossible to undo all the past hurts that have contributed to the vulnerable self, but it is possible to learn from them and to use the learning in the service of teaching and leadership.

	Known to self	Unknown to self	
Known to others	Open self	Unaware self	Known to others
Unknown to others	Secret self	Unconscious self	Unknown to others

Figure 6.1: The Johari Window (Luft, 1984)

The process of becoming fully aware and accepting of the vulnerable self involves a journey into past hurts to revisit the origins of vulnerability.[2] Hurt and shame are normally the products of damaging interpersonal relationships and therefore can be retriggered by certain situations or interpersonal dynamics that are reminiscent of the original injury. If a leader is to resist the temptation to lash out at someone who unwittingly treads on their vulnerable self or to retreat into an isolated, wounded position, then they must become intimately acquainted with this part of themselves.[3]

Exercise

1 Make a list of things you appear to do well at work but which you actually feel incompetent or inadequate about.
2 What aspects of your personality or lifestyle do you fear colleagues knowing about you?
3 Which of these emotions do you fear most in yourself at work? Ring all those that apply:

Anger	Anxiety	Arrogance	Complacency	Disapproval
Envy	Exhaustion	Fear	Grief	Hurt
Impatience	Irritability	Loneliness	Shame	Suspicion

4 Which of these emotions do you fear most in those you lead?

Anger	Anxiety	Arrogance	Complacency	Disapproval
Envy	Exhaustion	Fear	Grief	Hurt
Impatience	Irritability	Loneliness	Shame	Suspicion

5 Can you pinpoint a particular event or person that has caused you to fear these emotions in yourself and/or in others?
6 How have you kept fear of these emotions alive in yourself?
7 Is there any relationship between your answers to questions 1, 2 and 3?

Developing awareness of the fears and anxieties contained within the vulnerable self is essential to protect leaders from some of the emotional wounding that is intrinsic to the role (Ackerman and Maslin-Ostrowski, 2004). Indeed, a thorough awareness and acceptance of the vulnerable self enables leaders to bring more energy to the constructive tasks of leadership. Sarah not only accessed a personal coach to help her gain a sense of perspective on what was happening between herself and staff but also went for counselling:

> I had a coach and I took a counselling course – both of those helped me to understand that it wasn't all my fault ... that it was part of their grieving process. That did help me to take a step back but it wasn't ever easy. I felt threatened a lot of the time.

Sounds as if gaining that perspective really helped but wasn't enough. How did you deal with feeling threatened?

As part of the counselling course I had to go into counselling myself … it was really helpful having somewhere to cry about it all and having someone to help me make sense of why I felt so threatened … realised it was to do with what happened to me at primary school and why I became a primary teacher in the first place … so it was really enlightening and I learned to know the difference between what I feel now and old feelings from the past so they didn't make things worse than they were. (P–H–I)

Sarah used counselling to engage with her vulnerable self and coincidentally to clarify her sense of moral purpose. Learning to differentiate between emotional responses that are appropriate for the 'here and now' context and those that are rooted in the past, the 'then and now', is important not just for accurate responding but also for self care. If Catherine had embraced her vulnerable self, then she would have been less likely to dismiss others and act in such emotionally wounding and destructive ways.

The shadow self

The shadow, a psychological metaphor introduced by JM Barrie in the opening of *Peter Pan* and developed by Jung (1968), holds those dark rejected aspects of self, which may include some vulnerabilities, as well as positive undeveloped potential. In an effort to be socially acceptable to others, baser qualities, such as hypocritical behaviour, greed, ruthlessness and rage are banished out of awareness, where they continue to exist unsupervised! Periodically, however, they appear and propel the individual into situations that they would much rather avoid. This may involve behaviour that is atypical for the individual, such as when a gentle, loving person is suddenly and inexplicably overcome by rage or jealousy. Many leaders struggled to articulate any ways in which they might negatively impact on their pupils, colleagues or community. Instead, there was a tendency to engage in a deficit discourse which effectively blamed pupils, parents, staff and others for the problems faced by the school. This is in evidence in the following quote from the head of an infants school:

People on this estate have negative views of the school and see us as somewhere to dump their children for a few hours ... they do not really want to be involved ... we have tried everything. (IS–TL–FG)

A deficit view of community is also noted by the review of the Primary National Strategy, which highlights this process at work in schools in challenging circumstances and points to the need for leaders and teachers to take more responsibility for success and failure:

Some of the schools facing the most challenging of circumstances too easily apportion blame for low achievement to external factors, including the pupils themselves, rather than considering weaknesses in their own teaching and support. (Ofsted, 2005a: 31)

The shadow may also manifest in more pervasive, pernicious behaviour towards others. Leaders who have not examined their need for power and who therefore treat their staff as objects rather than as human beings are working from their shadow, as are those who create unnecessarily high hoops for staff to jump through to earn their performance related pay, and those who create inner circles of special, favoured colleagues and therefore exclude others from access to information and opportunities for professional development. Staff in three schools cited a range of repercussions as a result of questioning or challenging the head's decision making, including:

- extra assemblies to lead

- additional playground duties

- loss of free periods

- having personal mail opened.

Not surprisingly, such abuses of power do little to create a climate of trust or of staff feeling cared for.

Passive aggression, as in rumour-mongering and making snide remarks, manipulation, direct aggression and projection are the main means by which the shadow self manifests itself. In all cases it is calling for the individual to attend to the disowned attribute or emotion and integrate it into a more realistic and coherent view of self. Catherine's shadow, for example, will continue to create distress in her school until she recognises not only her own vulnerability but also her disowned rage, ruthlessness and contempt for those who are different from herself.

> ### Exercise
>
> Reflect back on your school age self ... recall your childhood home in as much detail as you can ... and your place within it ... notice your feelings as you remember coming home from school each day ... recall also the adults who were around for you ...
>
> Write a list of the significant adults in your life at the time you have just been remembering. As you write each person's name make a note as to whether they were nurturing or wounding for you.
>
> Write down what you learned from each person and how they continue to influence your life and your behaviour as a leader today.

The personal shadow has also been influenced by the cultural shadow and will include emotional responses to those who are culturally different. It is therefore imperative that individuals develop awareness of their cultural roots and the assumptions about self and others that are embedded in their psyche and that may have a profound effect on individuals and groups within the wider school community. Jonathon Jansen (2006) undertook an in-depth study of two white Afrikaner principals who had successfully changed their schools into racially and culturally inclusive institutions despite huge local opposition in post-apartheid South Africa. He discovered five distinguishing features of these principals, the second of which alludes to not only the personal shadow of the principal but also the collective shadow of a nation's past:

> ... these principals are keenly aware of their own limitations, their personal prejudices, and their troubled histories as white South Africans. They do not pretend that the past did not happen, or that their personal lenses are untainted by years of growing up as part of a privileged and dominant racial minority in an African country. (Jansen, 2006: 100)

Owning and accepting the less culturally and socially acceptable aspects of self can also help to recognise the shadow in others. Such awareness can help the leader to resist the temptation to respond defensively and find more enabling ways of making contact with 'toxic' colleagues and parents. Jansen's principals, for example, experienced the shadow at work in the negative responses of their communities to school change. However, their deep commitment to inclusion, and the support they received from members of the black community helped them to survive the emotional challenges of collective disapproval and sabotage.

The vulnerable and shadow self in action

> Care of the soul speaks to the longings we feel and to the symptoms that drive us crazy, but it is not a path away from shadow or death. A soulful personality is complicated, multifaceted, and shaped by both pain and pleasure, success and failure. Life lived soulfully is not without its moments of darkness and periods of foolishness. Dropping the salvational fantasy frees us up to the possibility of self-knowledge and self-acceptance, which are the very foundation of soul. (Moore, 1992: xiv)

In the previous chapter Lisa's need to be seen in a good light by the authority meant she made an error of judgement that wounded staff and pupils. Fortunately, Lisa was able to recognise how her desire to be perceived as a 'successful head teacher' could negatively affect her judgement and subsequently her self esteem as well as that of staff and pupils. She is not only aware of her pattern but also able to acknowledge and be honest about her imperfections and take responsibility for them. Winnicott (1965), a pediatrician and analyst, coined the phrase 'good enough mother', and his work stimulates valuable insights into what constitutes 'good enough leadership'. Leadership errors may for example, be understood as important milestones towards greater self awareness and connectedness with others. Lisa provides a valuable illustration of this process in action. In this case she took the opportunity to discuss the issues with staff and to work with them to clarify a principled way forward:

> Fortunately I realised that I had made a mistake and told staff that they shouldn't feel bad for something that I foolishly, was sort of drawn into and foisted on them. I let them know it was my fault and that I didn't want them to feel so demoralised by my foolishness. We've now made a decision that that is not going to be the most important measure. And if we don't hit our key stage results, what are they going to do, put us in prison? All we want to do is make sure that the children achieve a lot but not more than they're capable of … we're not going to over coach them. We're not going to put the children under stress. … We also live in the real world and we know that we are accountable … so there is a balance to be struck … and we are getting there in our own way now … It's constructive to have talked everything through together and it is making a difference to how they relate to me … they are much cheekier towards me now … more relaxed … which is a good thing and keeps me in check. … I use humour a lot and some staff are definitely feeling more comfort-

able turning it back on me since they realised that I am human too and can be honest about my weak spots. (P–H–I)

Lisa has enough awareness and inner strength to own her vulnerability and take responsibility for her error, working alongside her staff to resolve the difficulties they are all experiencing. An authentic way of being in relationship involves taking full responsibility for both the good and the bad things that happen in the school environment. The authentic leader is transparent and able to share openly not only facts and figures relevant to a situation but also their judgements, feelings and intentions. They are willing to be seen in their humanity, to appropriately show their vulnerability and to allow others to take a lead, to develop their own competence and authenticity.

A commitment to enhance self awareness requires the leader to give up self-bolstering rhetoric and engage in more rounded self appraisal based on accurate awareness of strengths and growing edges. Lisa's concern for her image and reputation in the local authority (LA) highlights an issue raised by staff in other schools. Such staff perceive that their head's need to be valued outside the school and to show the school in a good light to the LA leads to a tokenistic engagement with new initiatives. It is the perceived misrepresentation of the school's work and achievements that contributes to a loss of faith in the head's integrity. Several staff from Northpark Infant School, for example, recognise the intense pressures from the LA to raise standards and yet feel the head responds to these in ways that are less than helpful:

> Great external pressure [from LEA etc.] to provide average national attainments in an area of severe social/linguistic deprivation [+70% free school meals]. Bureaucratic overload – trying to do too many things at once and not really doing any one very well. Mismatch between head's reporting of our work and what we actually do – she is only interested in us looking good, rather than being good. The problem is she believes what she says and writes herself – she even sends us copies and we all know the truth – it makes me sad. (I–J–SWOT)

> It's always a bugbear with me … we play the game and doctor the figures well. Not to do with SATS … but like the amount of people who attend certain events etc. looks a lot higher on paper than it is in reality, so these things look really successful and as if this school is managing it all beautifully, where the truth is not quite like that. (I–D–FG)

> We dip in and out of projects. The really important tasks are given lip service. Paperwork is the most important thing. What actually happens is often distorted to prove a point. (I–S–SWOT)

Teachers throughout Northpark School are therefore aware of the head's shadow at work and of the real temptation to engage in forms of deception in order to survive the relentless pressures for change from the Local Authority. However, they are not comfortable with her approach and are angry that the head has settled for 'image management' rather than talking through the issues with staff and occasionally saying 'no' to the Authority.

> There's a lot of good things going on but I think we should say 'No we're not doing that', rather than making out we are doing it. I think that's bad. (I–TL–FG)

> One thing you have to be as a professional is honest about performance, even if we have apparently zero progress on something. Okay, so we got zero progress, let's try another way. It's far better to be like that and to be honest than to say 'look at the progress we've made here'. (I–TL–FG)

However, within a culture of league tables and fear of humiliation such practice is possibly widespread. As the evaluation of the Primary National Strategy found this is a characteristic of weak rather than strong leadership and is unlikely to fool those used to checking the rhetoric out against more than the paper trail:

> poor quality of self-evaluation, with too much assertion, too little evidence and judgements which are often overgenerous. (Ofsted, 2005a: 26)

Such leadership reflects an instrumental rather than an authentic use of self and reflects leadership dominated by 'shouldism' without the benefit of awareness. Julie, head of Northpark School appeared to have no awareness that her view of school climate differed so radically from that of all her staff.

> Staff are behind me all the way. We speak with one voice and that makes us highly effective with the children. (I–H–I)

Staff reported several attempts to challenge the head, all of which had been brushed aside. When an NQT spoke of her observations of being in the school her perceptions found unanimous agreement amongst colleagues:

Staff do not feel valued or appreciated in this school ... (head) finds it easy to pull people down, which she does on a daily basis but she does not build them up at all ... so everyone is frustrated. (I–J–FG)

In this case it appears that Julie is adept at keeping herself safe from her own fears and limitations by projecting her incompetence onto staff and putting them down. In blaming the ills of the school onto others her shadow is acting as a slide projector. Meanwhile she remains hidden in the projection room, probably protecting herself from the pain of owning any incompetence on her part. She avoids being in relationship with staff and parents, dismissing their voices as unimportant or misguided, whilst publicly asserting that they are working together as a whole community. Julie is inadvertently wounding staff and causing distress to others. She needs to be supported to take responsibility for her own behaviour. Julie may, however, have a sense of moral purpose, a worldview and an internal working model of leadership that make perfect sense to her and within which her thoughts and actions do not create any internal dissonance.

Internal working model of leadership

School leaders, teacher leaders and pupil leaders all have an internal working model of leadership. Young people grow up with cultural stories of leadership as articulated through fairy tales, myths, religious stories, animation and other forms of popular culture (Fouts et al., 2006). All these influence their fantasy world as they enact versions of heroic stories in their play and their relationships with one another. Direct forms of leadership are also experienced through their engagement with community organisations, church, mosque or temple and of course, school. The role modelling of community leaders, religious leaders, head teachers and teachers help a young person to develop and fine tune their understanding and appreciation of what constitutes good and poor leadership within their particular cultural context. It also teaches them what is expected by way of followership.

With maturation and experience in life and the workplace the individual's working model will be influenced and reshaped by new experiences, especially those that challenge the original model accepted in youth.

> **Exercise**
>
> Draw a lifeline to illustrate key influences on your journey towards leadership.
> Use each side of the line to differentiate between positive and negative influences. Consider people, popular culture, literature …

As one of a staff team on a university-based interpersonal skills for leadership module, I was introduced to an exercise designed to help MBA students clarify which of two leaders they would choose to guide them down the white water rapids of the Motu river on a raft, either: Buzz, an authoritarian, confident, loud, task focused leader whose leadership must be obeyed – mastery over the river is his goal; or Kiwi, a calm, quiet leader who follows the flow of the river, watching and listening for signs and who enables his followers to learn the art of listening and heeding the rhythm and pace of the river. Befriending nature and sharing leadership amongst team members are the hallmarks of Kiwi's style. In reality, of course, people inhabit a wide range of leadership styles, all of which have their place but many of which cause others to feel wounded.

> **Exercise**
>
> Which of these styles fit most comfortably with your personality and preferred mode of communication? Which of these would your colleagues most identify with their experience of you? How do you know?
>
> Coaching   *Try this*
> Affiliative   *People come first*
> Authoritative   *Come with me*
> Democratic   *What do you think?*
> Pace setting   *Do as I do*
>
> (Adapted from Goleman, 2000)

Personal culture

Differences between Buzz and Kiwi reflect different cultural perspectives and worldviews. Elsewhere, I have written of the importance of racial and cultural awareness for developing effective relationships between teachers and young people (Harris, 2003). I argued there that learning about other cultures, whilst an essential part of the curriculum, must be balanced by a thorough awareness and understanding of one's own culture and how that might affect one's way of being, teaching and relationships. Recently there has been an upsurge of interest in the relationship between leaders' personal lives, culture and identities and the educational context in which they work (Kington, 2006). Loder and Spillane (2006: 92) highlight how a leader's capacity to manage dilemmas and tensions in school is directly related to personal biography. Their focus is on understanding how leaders manage challenges whereas mine is on helping leaders pay 'careful attention to their past lives' in order to increase their awareness and self-understanding.

Pederson (1997) maintains that each individual has at least 1,000 cultural teachers that influence their way of being in the world. Whilst it would take a long time to develop an in-depth working knowledge of what has been learned or 'caught' from all these teachers, many of whom have been known vicariously via literature, films or stories, it is important to develop a thorough working knowledge of the influence of key family members and high status community members, such as priests, Immans, social leaders and so on. In this way it is possible to recognise some of the cultural messages that were introjected as a child and that have possibly never been subject to scrutiny. Such messages may have helped the younger self feel safe and connected to significant others sharing the same beliefs. However, they may also inhibit making meaningful and respectful relationships with people who are different.

Unexamined attitudes can play a powerful role in subtly condoning or promoting anti-social behaviour, such as name-calling, bullying or even violence between different sectors of the school population. Prejudice is part and parcel of being human and is indicative of the capacity to make choices and establish personal preferences in relation to theories, practices, behaviours and, of course, people. Prejudice per se only becomes problematic if it supports behaviours that treat the self (as in internalised homophobia or racism) or others as unworthy of respect and care, as objects rather than as people. It is important therefore to become aware of prejudices to ensure that leadership is executed with due regard for human difference. Effective leaders deliberately seek out relationships based on difference to make their schools and classrooms more inclusive, to expand their horizons and review how their assumptions and values are impacting on their judgement. Indeed, this is essential for the development of emotional maturity:

'The best hope of emotional maturity' says Christopher Lashe, 'appears to lie in a creative tension between separation and union, individuation and dependence. It lies in the recognition of one's need for and dependence on people who nevertheless remain separate from oneself and refuse to submit to one's whims'. (Dowrick, 1992: 51)

Exercise – Explore your cultural roots

How would you describe your family culture when you were growing up? What were important family sayings?

Who were your cultural 'heroes' – the people who influenced you and who you looked up to most? What did they teach you about yourself and your place in the world?

Do you remember the first time you became aware of people as different by virtue of their
• gender?
• skin colour?
• disability?
• sexual orientation?
• religion?
• other differences?

What happened and what was that like for you? How do you account for that within your family culture?

How were people who did not follow your family's way of being and living referred to in your family of origin? What effect did these messages have on you?

What, if anything has happened in your life to reinforce or challenge these messages about differences?

Closing thoughts

The formal leader and teacher leader needs to develop and fine tune his or her here-and-now awareness of self and of self-in-relationship with adults and young people. Such self-awareness and understanding can be developed in many ways such as through training in group work skills (Harris and Biddulph, 2000), human relations (Hall et al., 1988), counselling (Hall et al., 1996), focusing (Gendlin, 1978) or meditation (Kabat-Zinn, 1994). Whichever approach is most accessible or preferable, it will involve some movement out of the comfort zone and into unknown territory to explore personal ways of meaning making and how past experience of authority, for example, has shaped their way of being and their internal working model of leadership. They will need to become acquainted with their vulnerability and rigorously examine their need for power and control over others, their capacity for self deception and the ways in which they interrupt their own cycle of experience and therefore carry unfinished business into the school, which may negatively impact on their relationships with others. Without respect for the self, there can be no genuine respect for the other and therefore it is incumbent upon leaders and teachers to develop awareness of self as a prerequisite for authentic and effective relationships with others.

> A leader's deepest obligation is to engage continually in a reflective process of making sense of his or her leadership and to trust its influence on others and on the school. (Ackermann and Maslin-Ostrowski, 2004: 32)

It is essential to stay open to self-doubts, fears and questions, to submit dearly held beliefs, feelings and preoccupations to review and scrutiny and to learn to trust the inner world. It is also important to reflect on Marianne Willamson's words (quoted by Nelson Mandela in his inaugural speech) that remaining fearful may reflect an avoidance of personal power:

> Our deepest fear is not that we are inadequate. Our deepest fear is that we are powerful beyond measure. It is our light, not our darkness that most frightens us. We ask ourselves, 'Who am I to be brilliant, gorgeous, talented, fabulous?' Actually, who are you not to be? We are all meant to shine as children do ... and as we let our own light shine, we unconsciously give other people permission to do the same. As we are liberated from our own fear, our presence automatically liberates others. (Williamson, 1992: 190–1)

Endnotes

[1] Lipman-Blumen defines toxic leaders as 'those individuals who by dint of their *destructive behaviours* and *dysfunctional personal qualities* generate a serious and enduring poisonous effect on the individuals, families, organisations, communities, and even entire societies they lead' (2005: 29).

[2] This involves a move beyond the comfort zone and is therefore best undertaken with adequate support systems.

[3] Recovery from a wound, and the ability to transcend the wound, requires insight and reflection to understand the experience and be able to use the experience to help others. Wounded healers are able to transform their wound into a positive experience by being open to the possibility, recognising, questioning and, eventually, consciously using the experience (Conti-O'Hare, 2002). If the wound is not transcended, the individual becomes one of the 'walking wounded', that is, the wound may be recognised but there may be an inability to understand its effect, or to transcend the wound (Myss, 1997). Parse (1992) views healing as a process of 'becoming' and part of the normal rhythm of life. Wounded healer theories encompass the notion that the whole is greater than the sum of its parts (Conti-O'Hare, 2002).

7 *Values: a process approach*

Introduction

Cameron, a bright year 7 student at a Catholic comprehensive school, had arrived from a secular multi-cultural, multi-racial primary school and found the mono-cultural focus of Religious Education lessons in sharp contrast to the multicultural, inclusive culture of his primary school. Having had a humanist rather than a religious upbringing he felt at a disadvantage in relation to his peers. Inquisitive, and not wanting to be perceived as ignorant, he asked his mother to buy him a simplified copy of the bible and proceeded to familiarise himself with bible stories.

On one particular day, Brendan, a newly qualified Religious Education teacher who was being observed by his university mentor, was encouraging pupils to examine the relationship between bible messages and the rules governing personal behaviour in school. He set a small group task in which pupils were asked to match specific school rules with a number of bible stories. After a while a heated exchange began in Cameron's group. When Brendan stopped the discussion and asked the group what was happening, group members indicated that Cameron had a problem. Cameron began by saying that the exercise made him want to disregard school rules rather than follow them. He explained that some bible stories could lead to bad behaviour and therefore directly contradict school rules. He cited the school rule 'Everyone should be treated with respect, regardless of gender, race and ability', a comment which Brendan found puzzling:

B: I don't understand what the problem is, Cameron. There are lots of examples of Jesus demonstrating respect for people regardless of who they are.

C: Yes, Sir. But do you really believe that we should behave as the Bible says?

B: Yes, of course I do.

C: So ... [pause] do you think homosexuality is wrong then, Sir? [Giggles in the classroom].

B: Well, according to the Bible it is ...

C: But what do *you* think, Sir?

B: It's not my place to give you my opinion. I'm here to teach you about the Bible.

C: Are you saying that it's good behaviour if people stone a man to death for sleeping with another man? Do you think it is okay to kill people for being homosexual?
        [Giggles and sniggering throughout the class].

B: No, not literally ...

C: So we shouldn't always do what it says in the Bible then?

B: Cameron, that's enough. Please leave the class and wait outside the head teacher's office.

As he leaves the class, several kids whisper 'gay boy', 'bumboy' and so on, loud enough for everyone to hear and causing a ripple of laughter across the class. It takes Brendan five minutes to bring the class to order.

Exercise

What is your reaction to this story?

What are the ethical issues facing the teacher. The mentor?

If you were the teacher's mentor how would you debrief Brendan?

What do you think needs to happen next?

If you were the head teacher how would you respond to Cameron?

Would it make a difference if you knew that Cameron's godparents were a gay couple who took an active and loving interest in his personal and educational development?

Fortunately, both Cameron and Brendan managed to repair the rupture in their relationship and Brendan was proactive in ensuring that any students displaying a homophobic attitude through their bullying behaviour towards Cameron were quickly stopped in their tracks. Cameron's strong sense of self, his love for his godparents and his humanitarian values helped him to survive the taunting without any long-lasting damage. However, in the discussion between Brendan and his mentor, it emerged that Brendan was unaware of how his own behaviour might undermine pupils' trust and willingness to work within the parameters of the school's values. He was aware of judging the head teacher and senior colleagues on whether they 'walked the talk' but had not recognised the parallel in his relationships with young people. Brendan thought that teaching young people values was important but had no sense of himself as embodying the school's values in his way of being in the classroom.

In the early chapters of this book I discussed the impact of globalisation on individuals, relationships, communities and schools. I argued that the growing sense of alienation, fragmentation and loss of direction is reflected in the behaviour of staff and young people in schools. Loss of faith in the system and cynicism in the face of empty rhetoric is rife. It is therefore imperative that school leaders and leaders of learning recognise the key role they play in challenging cynicism and apathy in order to support colleagues' and pupils' engagement in learning and develop a sense of community.

The literature on teacher stress and school exclusion are replete with examples of teachers and pupils who feel invisible and missed, in that no one seems to care or want to take any responsibility for helping sort out the problems that have led to their stress or poor behaviour and who furthermore construe them as a problem rather than as people responding to particular conditions in the field. To many, the espoused values of care and respect for everyone, which Cameron picked up on in class, seem to apply to everyone else! In this way schools reinforce negativity, an 'us and them', 'insiders and outsiders' mentality, whilst talking the language of respect, care and empowerment. It is little wonder that some teachers and some schools make some young people very angry.

Trust

Re-establishing trust in teachers, in leadership and in schools involves not just agreeing a vision or a set of school values but ensuring that these values are embodied in the behaviours of all staff and therefore experienced as predictable and consistent over time. This is especially important for those young people who are suffering the effects of traumatic stress and/or have little experience or expectation of stable, caring and secure attachment relationships with adults. In schools where values and values education are embedded into school life and embodied by teachers and leaders there is evidence of improvement in pupils' self confidence, pro-social behaviour (Alexander and Thomas, 2004) and capacity for leadership (Hart et al., 2004). When the experience of school or leadership challenges an individual's expectations and therefore inhibits the normal pattern of responding, and there is enough psychological safety to facilitate experimentation with new ways of thinking and being, and these efforts are valued and appreciated, then trust is more likely to be engendered and change more likely to occur. One example of this in action is the CATE[1] project where a group of secondary schools, LA staff (Education Welfare Officer, Educational Psychologist), Connexions service and Youth Offending Team coordinate their efforts to support pupils at risk of exclusion. Evidence from the CATE evaluation study highlights how a fresh start based on more caring pupil-centred relationships and learning opportunities led to a significant reduction in problem behaviour and attendance as well as a range of other outcomes identified by both parents and pupils. These included better relationships at home, a more positive attitude towards school and increased motivation to engage in activities, both at school and at home. Pupils attributed these changes to new forms of relationship with teachers that offered consistency of approach and appropriate scaffolding of learning:

> The teachers [are better here]. Like here you get stages. If you mis-behave you get stage 1 and then if you carry on you get stage 2 and if you carry on some more you get stage 3 and you have to go see X and then if you carry on after that you get stage 4 and you have to leave the lesson. They didn't have anything like that at Y. (S–P–I)

> When I first started going into lessons they gave me different work to everybody else that were a bit easier. So I'd be able to go straight through that and then they put me on harder work and I'd do that. And then they put me on a bit harder work until I'm the same as everyone in the class. (S–P–I)

Sustaining such environments however, can be difficult, particularly in those schools with 'serious weaknesses' or under threat of amalgamation or closure, or with temporary leadership and teaching arrangements. Brian Caldwell (2006) argues that schools which establish collaborative networks of pupils, teachers and leaders offer a viable and effective means of supporting ongoing change with 'moral purpose'. One member of the CATE Pupil Placement Panel illustrates how the peer process sharpens the moral dimension of accountability:

> They have to present a case, not to parents; not to a governor ... but to colleagues in other schools ... So they think twice and make sure it's right and that you're doing the right thing. Schools won't say that because I don't think they are actually brave enough to say that they have changed what they are doing. I actually think they have because of dealing with colleagues. I also believe the schools have been made to reassess [the kids]. (PRU–D–I)

Certainly, in this cluster of schools the number of exclusions decreased significantly during the first year of the CATE protocol, with more young people receiving focused preventative provision. Matching a range of provision to the specific needs of the young person both in and out of school was highlighted by the university evaluators as a strength of the programme (Thomson et al., 2006). Interestingly, several of the young participants were aware of feeling different once they became CATE pupils. It is as if their being the centre of attention at the Pupil Placement Panel filters down through the system to give them a sense of being cared for and respected. This is then directly experienced through their relationships with teachers, especially those who were welcoming and supportive of their needs:

> We had one visit to Mr X (head) and then he rang up the same day and said: 'We'll accept you' and I started school straight away. (S–P–I)

> Most teachers (at my last school) they just shout at you, don't they? And you listen better when they talk to yer. I thought 'if they don't respect me then why should I respect them'. The teachers here want to help yer. They want what's best for yer. They gave me extra support ... they helped yer more than everyone else. (S–P–I)

> He really didn't want to come here at the start but now he's really glad that he has. He really loves this place and he's grateful for what they've done for him. At times he's done really well and there have been things that have happened since he's been here that have made him feel so good about himself. (S–Parent–I)

These expressions of appreciation and willingness to experiment with new ways of behaving and learning are indicative of feeling and believing that they matter (Harris, Vincent et al., 2006). These pupils began to trust their teachers and their schools, and by extension themselves. This trust enabled them to take in the care and positive reflections of themselves mirrored back by staff, peers and parents. They began to believe in themselves, to let go of their façade, risk connection with their teachers and express appreciation for their care and support.

Although it would be wrong to give the impression that pupils at all schools received the same quality of relationships and care, or responded as well to the opportunities they were afforded, in those cases where pupils' needs were made a priority and pupils took the space and opportunity to develop new skills and new relationships with teachers and peers, so-called 'disaffected', 'difficult' and 'abnormal' young people settled, blossomed and achieved beyond expectations. CATE has certainly 'done the right thing' by them.

At no point during the research did teachers or LA staff mention values and it was not clear what explicitly stated values, if any, were shared across the schools. Perhaps some attention to this matter would have reduced the discrepancy in the experience of a minority of pupils. However, the care, attention and detail afforded each pupil's case by the Pupil Placement Panel and the staff development opportunity this offered its members have had an impact on provision in schools and on pupils' lives. As one member says:

> On the panel you build up a picture ... every school has to be different. It can be useful to be aware of these differences. I also think personalities are important and I sometimes think, 'If I can get him in front of such a teacher that will be good' and, of course the other way round. (PRU–D–I)

Having thought about how embodied values and collaboration across schools can make a difference to some pupils it is important to consider how values interface with leadership.

Values and Leadership

In his seminal study on leadership James MacGregor Burns (1978) drew attention to the universal craving for 'compelling and creative leadership' to engage people at all levels of organisational life. He highlighted the particular importance of moral leadership as a way of meeting peoples' most basic needs. This ethical dimension to leadership is often described as 'moral purpose', as if it constituted a permanent and fixed phenomenon. In reality, however, an aware leader's sense of moral purpose reflects a composite of different values, or 'stars by which I navigate my life' (Hopson and Scally, 1981). Values are forged through a combination of personal narrative (what is it in the personal story of the leader that has brought them into education and influenced their journey into leadership – often an emotionally charged event), professional influences and beliefs (theories and experiences that have shaped the leader's thinking, for example distributed leadership, networking) and the process of experiential learning, of being fully aware in the moment of a particular constellation of circumstances and of the possible consequences of different courses of action. Polster and Polster highlight how enhanced awareness is central to this process:

> ... awareness is a continuous means for keeping up to date with one's self. It is an ongoing process, readily available at all times ... like an underground stream, ready to be tapped into when needed, a refreshing and revitalising experience. Furthermore, focusing on one's awareness keeps one absorbed in the present situation, heightening the impact of ... common experience in life. With each succeeding awareness one moves closer to articulating the themes of ones own life and closer also to moving towards the expression of these themes. (1973: 211–12)

In other words, values are constantly under the leader's microscope as they respond authentically and energetically to each and every encounter with individuals and events within the school. Certainly pupils, colleagues and parents are astute in recognising the difference between avowed and enacted values, between a leader's words and actions.

Exercise

What are the stories in your life that propelled you into education and into leadership? Consider points in your life that had deep meaning for you, such as

- moments of disruption, adversity, disappointment ...
- moments of joy, enlightenment, inner peace ...

How did these moments affect you emotionally and how did they affect your thinking? How did you deal with the challenge?

Imagine yourself telling one of these stories to colleagues and one to pupils – which would you choose? What feelings would you hope to engender? What impression of you would you want them to take away?

Most theories of moral development are based on rationalist, cognitive perspectives and yet there is a considerable body of evidence to suggest that emotions play the larger role in decision making. Haidt (2001) described emotions as gatekeeper to the moral world and indicated that the capacity to healthily integrate reason, emotion, intuition and social factors is important for moral acuity. In other words, developing awareness of emotional 'gut' responses to situations is an important starting point in moral leadership, a view supported by Green et al. (2001). Whilst participants were involved in solving ethical dilemmas, researchers used neuro-imaging techniques to analyse brain activity. They found that the brain region involved in emotional processing (particularly those areas associated with grief and fear) was over-active when participants considered moral dilemmas involving directly hurting a person.

In reality, there are no moral truths but plenty of preferences and values that guide decision making. Ethical and moral dilemmas are rarely straightforward as any decision may benefit some people more than others and therefore cause more distress in the system. This is of course particularly true in schools with pupils from a wide range of ethnic, religious, political and economic backgrounds and where many of the assumptions and 'givens' of school life have to be renegotiated on a daily basis. Teachers, parents and community often judge leaders by how they act in a crisis and whether they are seen to stand up for what is deemed to be good, true and right. They are often unaware of the internal struggle that has preceded any particular course of action and therefore may be quick to judge outcomes without due consideration of the complexities or effort involved. They may also not care about the impact of particular decisions on some sections of the school community. The school must therefore support robust relationships between colleagues, governors and parents that enable these difficult and sensitive ethical conversations to take place so that wisdom can be developed and shared amongst community members for the benefit of the school:

> One becomes a wise practitioner by practicing being wise. It may thus be domain specific: The wise teacher may not be a wise parent. Relatedly, wisdom honors the priority of the particular, i.e., it is sensitive to the importance of context. It requires detailed knowledge of the other people involved in a situation. (Sharpe and Schwartz, 2006: 388)

From this perspective conversations about ethics and morality are essential building blocks on a school's journey towards shared leadership and community engagement. Pupils, parents, governors, teachers and leaders all need opportunities to participate in robust discussions about the issues that affect their lives. They also need to know that their feelings and opinions count and contribute to the process of moving things forward.

A moral/ethical institution is one which creates authentic, caring, nurturing and healthy communities in which people can organise their lives for the development of their full potential and serve the common good both individually and collectively. Csikszentmihalyi (1993: 162) highlights the importance of harmony as a guiding force in developing healthy institutions. From his perspective harmony is achieved by organisational change that increases both differentiation (the degree to which a system is composed of parts that differ in function and structure) and integration (how different parts communicate and enhance one another's goals). He highlights the need for a 'moral code' to govern all interactions and ensure that potential conflicts can be contained. However, moral codes can also be limiting and it might be more useful to consider a values framework based on different fundamental and interrelated values and personal moral qualities of the practitioner. A framework recognises the complexity of many moral dilemmas and allows for discussion from different perspectives. Such a framework might include:

- Respect – for self and others
- Integrity – being true to self and others
- Responsibility – to self and others
- Cooperation – awareness and appreciation of others
- Patience – with self, others and events
- Beneficence – desire to promote wellbeing in self and others.

Exercise

1 Is there anything you would want to add to this, about the values that are most important to you as a leader?

2 Re-read any of the vignettes in this book. Use the values framework to consider what is happening using this framework.

In some cases, however, a values framework might not be sufficient to break the deadlock between stakeholders for whom other values are more important. Paul Pederson (2000) discusses this issue in relation to cross-cultural conflict, whether between individuals, groups or nations and highlights some of the real tensions that can exist between different cultural groups if conversation stays at the level of what constitutes acceptable actions and behaviour. Cross-cultural conflict, he argues, is best resolved in these cases by examining the common ground of expectations. The following exercise is designed to encourage discussion and debate between different stakeholders in order to identify some common ground expectations.

Small group exercise

Work in small groups comprised of different voices in the school community, i.e. a middle leader group, a parents group, etc. Each group has 30 minutes in which to create an image or symbol to represent their view of the 'ideal school'.

This should include consideration of how each of these should look/feel:
• School environment – internal and external
• School organisation – power structures/rules/procedures
• Relationships – internal and external
• Discipline – e.g. strict, assertive, relaxed
• Teaching and learning – e.g. didactic, cooperative, experiential.

Each group puts up its image to create a picture gallery for other members to look at – without discussing or explaining. Original groups re-form to talk through their impressions of what they noticed and how that made them feel.

Each group then has five minutes to present their expectations about how each of these aspects of school life would be, look, feel, etc.

Whole group discussion to identify at least one point of common ground related to each of the above areas.

How can you hold onto these expectations and use them as a guide to interactions between different stakeholders in the future?

The Leader's Values

In the MEAZ schools, the leaders who were most trusted and valued by staff were perceived as leading from the 'inside out' rather than the 'outside in'. In each case staff had a good idea, for example, of what made them tick, what excited them, what drove them, what values they espoused and what goals they had in life and for the school. Most importantly, staff experienced their leaders as congruent, as saying what they mean and meaning what they say. Sam, for example, describes herself 'at heart I'm a teacher rather than a manager' and staff are vocal in their appreciation for how much cover Sam does in the school to support their professional development:

> It's important to Sam that children are ready to learn and able to learn effectively because we tend to their emotions and what's happening to them at home … she knows we're effective but she cares about improving how we do it in the classroom, so we're encouraged to go on courses and if we want to go on a course then Sam does a lot of cover so it can happen and be shared out between us. (I–TL–FG)

> She's not one of those heads that hides away – she loves teaching and she's really good at it. (I–J–FG)

Sam also identifies involving parents in the life of the school as a key value:

> We definitely try to do a lot more parental involvement since I've been here because it's something that's very dear to my heart, probably as dear as anything. (I–H–I)

And once more this is known and understood by her staff:

> I don't know how she does all the cover she does except that it's so important to her that the kids and the parents get a good deal. Her husband and her daughter are teachers too – it's like it's in her genes [laughter and nodding]. (I–TL–FG)

Sam has evolved a clear sense of her own purpose and direction over many years of headship. She herself was keen to point out that the process of searching has been more valuable than reaching any destination. It is the journey into the existentialist self that she cites as most formative:

> I don't think I started out with a vision or a clear set of values, just a determination to do the best job I could and to be the best I could be with the knowledge, skills, experience and personality I had at that time. They were not however, adequate to the task and there have been many times when I have wondered what I am doing and

whether I can go on … but then I have a break and I get some perspective back, or something good happens and I think 'That's why I am here. That's my purpose.' So it's as if my purpose has found me rather than me finding it sometimes … and I have learned to be more generous to myself and to my staff. They work extremely hard and give a lot and I know I do push them to keep learning and growing as people because that is important to me … now I can honestly say the suit is beginning to fit and that is a source of joy … and sometimes even of peace [laughs] … but it is the learning and growing that are most rewarding and that keep me firmly planted in the classroom and in the lives of these children and their families.

Exercise

What is it that makes your heart sing at work?

What does it mean to you to live a good and moral life?

What are the 'stars by which you navigate your life'?

How do you wish to be remembered when you have left your school – by pupils and by colleagues?

What do you hope to leave as a legacy to your pupils and colleagues?

Values, ethics and leadership in action

Creating an ethical school therefore involves evolving a culture of sharing, of developing and reviewing goals, expectations and mechanisms for decision making. Such cultures are founded on caring:

This school has a very happy ethos generally and that's something we have worked towards and really fostered as a whole group. It's not just the teachers but absolutely everybody helps towards making it a happy environment for the pupils and anybody coming in … everybody looks out for one another and that kind of ethos is a very caring ethos … and I think it's something that when you do go through the door you do tend to see that … but that's taken time to build up that kind of environment and that kind of feeling … [head] has helped us to do that by her attention to each and everyone of us. (SS–TL–I)

Everyone at Park Special School understands how they contribute to the ethos and well being of the children, including the kitchen staff:

> Getting the happiness I feel about working here through to the children (SS–Kitchen Staff–SWOT)

> Children do come in with all sorts of emotional baggage, especially the teenage end of the school. There's always somebody, whether it's support staff or even a dinner lady, anybody. There's always somebody here to help. And I think that's what I feel is very important, that ethos … I think the pupils feel quite secure in it. (SS–TL–I)

In this school the head teacher's story of her experience as a mother of a child with a medical condition has driven her decision to work in Special Education and her leadership style.

> When my son was six years old his asthma became chronic and he had to spend some months in hospital. I was teaching full-time in a secondary school … I know that one of the pressures I faced as a working mother of a sick child was that the hospital staff would make demands of me, 'You'll need to come in and give your child his inhaler' or 'If you want your child to participate in swimming (or whatever) then you'll have to be with him' and I found it very stressful. Now I spend a lot of time listening to parents trying to make myself accessible. Before I had the delights of sitting on the children's ward at the (hospital) I would have had a different response. Now, if a child is a bit poorly, upset or distressed, I'll say 'You just stay here and rest', whereas before I would have said 'come on – just go out to play – you'll be okay' and I try to encourage staff to … always think 'how would you feel to have a child with special needs or short life expectancy?' … we've had our fair share of children who died. That is something you never get used to – it's a highly emotional place – it's not a sad place … We make a point of visiting a child in hospital or saying to a parent 'shall we come over before school so you can go home to have your breakfast or clean your teeth without eyes looking at you. It's really important. (SS–H–I)

Ethical leadership is therefore founded on a fundamental consideration of how we would like to be treated in similar circumstances. Such 'practical wisdom' (Sharpe and Schwartz, 2006) involves no small amount of will to find and implement the right course of action in morally complex situations. It is rooted in human integrity and requires a particular kind of responsiveness, based on openness to the 'other', whether teacher, child or parent; being willing to imagine what it might feel like to be in the other person's shoes, and on a willingness to find creative solutions to new and complex dilemmas and problems. This is illustrated by Sarah, who is involved in a difficult process with a member of her staff:

> I've got a capability procedure. It's one of the hardest things I've had to do. And you can only cope with knowing you are putting that person through it for the sake of the children. That's the only way you can square it in your mind to give you the strength. (I–H–I)

Although driven by a deep commitment to the education of children in her school, Sarah maintains an empathic awareness of the potential for shame and disgrace and is keen to avoid this for her teacher:

> Emotionally it's not so hard for me as the person who's going through it. I know that if I'd had my teaching ability criticised by two heads I would have been under and never wanted to put my head above the parapet again. (I–H–I)

This combination of self and other awareness, combined with a willingness to balance needs and principles and a capacity to communicate care and concern can help individuals and groups understand and work with the complex dynamics of a situation. Once shared expectations have been established, people can normally relax some of their rigidity and accept different means to reach mutually agreed end goals. This ability requires the leader to have a 'process orientation', a dual focus on the 'how' and the 'what' of classroom and school experience.

Awareness of process in action

> In a process orientation everything is energy (movement, action), is structured by the dynamic forces of the field, and moves through time and space. Just as field treats phenomena as a continuous whole rather than treating discrete particles, it treats the field as in motion rather than static .... Everything changes. Even that which appears static is in fact changing over time. (Yontef, 1993: 313)

The process-oriented leader, teacher or helper is not only committed to their own awareness and internal personal process but also to the processes at work within the field of the classroom or school. They recognise that everything is in flux and in the process of becoming, evolving and changing. English and English describe process as:

> A change or a changing in an object or organism in which a consistent quality or direction can be discerned. A process is always in some sense active; something is happening. It contrasts with the *structure* or form of organisation of what changes, which structure is conceived to be relatively static despite process change. (1958: 410)

If we accept this field theoretical position that change is inevitable, that there is an underlying order to change and that things change whether leaders intervene or not, then the key issue is how to use the self as leader to support constructive, life-enhancing change and to prevent things changing for the worse!

The process-oriented leader knows that the very systems and processes they develop at the operational level of their school, department, classroom or kitchen and the way in which decisions are made, will play a significant role in people's experience of the school environment. As Jay, head of Park Special School says:

> My style of leadership is very much 'hands-on'. It is important that I'm seen regularly around the school, spend a lot of time in classrooms, have a teaching commitment and so lead from the front. I enjoy it but also I know exactly what problems they're facing and can respond quickly. It's humbling to realise how what I've considered to be really good new initiatives or ideas can actually make things more difficult for staff ... so I pride myself on experiencing first hand what something feels like on the ground. That way I know what problems they're facing pretty quickly so we can return to the drawing board together and find better ways of resolving some of the problems we face. (H–SS–I).

Jay therefore perceives herself alongside her staff, students and their families and recognises that they are all engaged in a continual and creative process of making sense of different facets or aspects of themselves-in-their-environment in order to create new meaning and understanding. This view of individuals as active agents and leaders of their own lives within the particular field conditions of the school at any one point in time is central to a process-oriented understanding of school life. Any aspect of a person's behaviour therefore can be understood as a manifestation of the gestalt or whole, rather than as a mere manifestation of the individual's pathology. The individual is perceived and received as a person worthy of respect for their particular perspective on events.

A process-oriented school leader will work to ensure that the internal organisation of the school maximises possibilities for communication and collaboration between different interest groups (pastoral, academic, administrative) and stakeholders (students, parents, governors, staff). The effects of Jay's awareness of the relationship between her own behaviour and of staff perceptions of school climate are reflected and supported by staff confidence in her and in the system. Most importantly, Jay's process orientation helps staff feel cared for and valued:

> We're managed very well. We're backed up well on all our projects ... She walks the job and makes us feel valued. (SS–TL–FG)

This sense of being valued is perceived by Jay as central to staff feeling safe enough to ask her for help. It is also a reminder of the importance of humility and being willing to own up to mistakes:

> The staff seem to appreciate my involvement and my willingness to own up to my misjudgements ... I think it has helped develop a culture where people feel able to say to me 'I'm struggling ... I need help', and for that to be okay. We all need help sometimes and it's my job to make sure they get what they need so they can give their full attention to the children. (SS–TL–FG)

Again, her self awareness proves to be accurate in that staff volunteer a similar view of her during the focus group:

> [Jay] always makes time to chat, so it's easy to let her know if you have a problem with a class or a particular pupil and she's very supportive ... and she's also flexible when you are sick or whatever. She covered my class for me so I could take my daughter to hospital and she really cared about what happened to us as a family. I never

expected that from a head teacher and I think that has helped me to realise how important it is to put myself out for others. (SS–JS–I)

Indeed, within the focus group discussion there is unanimous agreement amongst staff that Jay's consistent and caring leadership style helped to create a whole school environment in which staff feel safe enough to be honest and open with one another and to discuss difficult or sensitive issues. Moreover, it is this experience of honest sharing that reinforces a sense of being valued as a whole person:

> We have whole school meetings where you're able to express yourselves and if there's a problem you're able to talk about it without feeling 'oh I'm going to get into trouble over this'. If there are issues you can talk about them and because you can talk about them you feel that you are valued. (SS–JS–FG)

There is a clear relationship here between Jay's presence, caring and non-judgemental attitude in school and the staff's sense of feeling accepted and valued as people. These attributes are also essential in helping to manage the external boundary of the school or classroom to minimise the amount of disturbance or shaking to the core activity of teaching and learning and manage stress levels within the total organisation. In the case of Park Special School, for example, changes in government policy towards inclusion and a long-term threat of closure could have seriously affected staff morale and well being. Jay, however, has a strong sense of the inevitability of change and takes this in her stride. Moreover, she recognises the staff development opportunities afforded by an intensification of the threat of closure. She therefore engaged in the Education Action Zone's emotional intelligence initiative as a means of enabling staff to express their feelings. In taking this approach she is aware of the relationship between staff and pupils' emotional well being:

> As a school we are supportive of inclusion but there's also a feeling that it is emotionally challenging for many ... our numbers are being cut and I'm losing £65,000 off my budget so staff are going to have to come to terms with that and that our capacity as a school is changing. Ultimately we could be looking long term at closure. That's something that's always in the background. This school has been closing ever since I came here ten years ago ... . For some of

the staff, they love being here and it's really hard for them, it's hard for them to come to terms with ... so the emotional intelligence work just helps to legitimate us talking about these matters and helps people to express how they really feel. It's important that they don't sit on their feelings. They need to be able to help the children with their feelings ... but how can they hear them unless they can express their own? (SS–H–I)

Jay's awareness of the interconnectedness of the staff, student and parent experience underpins her leadership and is perceived as central to the ethos of the whole school:

When she took over as head three years ago we were in a mess and everyone was distressed about being placed in special measures. From the moment she took over as acting head we started to feel differently. Her positive attitude and her faith in us helped us to gradually believe in ourselves and the importance of what we are doing. There are no cliques or favourites here ... everyone is important. I feel really fortunate to have such a competent human being for a head. Her care for her staff and for her pupils and their families is something we have all been infected by ... it feels like a real privilege to work here – especially when I hear my friends talking about their schools! I just keep quiet and count my blessings. (SS–TL–I)

Pupils echoed these feelings of belonging and of everyone being important, irrespective of the severity of their medical condition. One pupil recognises that the size of the school contributes to this when she says 'everybody knows who you are so it's like being in a big family where everyone looks out for everyone.' Other pupils highlighted the approachability and warmth of all staff, including the site manager and cook:

Neil:	It's not just the teachers who's nice. Absolutely everyone's nice in this school.
Luke:	One thing that makes me safe is the teachers.
Interviewer:	All of them?
Luke:	All the people.
Heena:	And J [cook] as well.
Neil:	S and R [site manager/driver].

Pat: And also the supply teachers.

Sarah: We're all special here.

Some readers will be concerned that such personal caring and presence may be achievable within a small special school context but be unmanageable within a large secondary school. There is no doubt that such personal and process-centred ways of engaging could exact a huge personal cost as the leader shoulders the burden of external demands, directives and information and seeks creative ways of brokering relationships between various stakeholders. In addition, they need to proactively respond to specific issues or events arising within and from the process of collective meaning making in the school. Mel, head of a large secondary school involved in IQEA, had engaged in emotional literacy training and was proactively seeking to apply the learning to her school. She identified her new-found awareness of process as a source of renewed energy and hope:

> I just feel I am trying to experiment without fear of failure. If something does fail then there must be a better way of doing it to make it better, rather than giving up or colluding with staff or students giving up, so I feel it's kind of hopeful. ... I hope that my responding this way will rub off on staff and filter through to help them as they take risks and introduce new teaching and learning strategies in the classroom ... so they take failure more in their stride and don't give up either ... (S–H–I)

Interestingly a number of staff mentioned significant changes in Mel following her training, stating that they felt more relaxed and less fearful than before. One male member of the focus group offered an example that seems to substantiate Mel's claims:

> ... people have actually said that 'when I try, I have tried this method of teaching and it did not work, for some reason or other it just was not successful'. So they are not afraid to actually say that they had been unsuccessful and they also said 'well I am going to try it another time and see if it works better with a different group'. So people are quite willing to verbalise their failures without any sort of retribution or being called ... These are old established teachers like myself. 'Old', in inverted commas, established members of staff are saying this. So that is good. I feel that it's a very positive point for staff to be able to say that. That is really new and says a lot about how far we've come. (S–TL–FG)

It may be argued that taking a process-oriented approach to leading change can reduce stress and enhance resilience if one is able to hold awareness of self. These benefits can have a positive, vicarious effect on staff well being and morale.[2] Within the psychological literature this capacity to stay with and trust the process is essential for good mental health:

> Health, radically understood, is simply a question of staying with the situated experiential process just as it presents itself, and letting the spontaneous play of energies flow freely, not separated by conflict into subject and object, inner and outer, myself and others, nor myself (here) and the situation (there). The wholesome flow, or creative interplay of the process is what principally matters. (Levin, 1981: 83)

Given the high levels of stress experienced by teachers and leaders I would argue that a focus on process brings a degree of perspective based on consideration of both the internal and external domains. This additional data enables the individual to feel more knowledgeable and confident about themselves and the decisions they make. However, a process-centred way of being is not sustainable without a thorough awareness and understanding of one's internal process and how this might positively and negatively affect the leader's capacity for honest and accurate self assessment.

Noticing process

Recall a recent conversation, meeting or classroom session that you have a keen memory of. Alternatively, make a deliberate effort to notice the process within the next conversation, meeting or teaching session. It is probably easier to do this if the occasion has some emotional content.

In your mind's eye listen carefully to the content ... the 'what?' of the experience ... notice what is happening ... who is there? ... what is being said? ... Notice the environment ...

Now move your attention from the 'what?' to the 'how?' of it.

Describe what you are noticing as the 'how?' ... allow your awareness to act as a searchlight ... notice what stands out in your memory ... recall the texture of the communication between individuals ... the tone of voice, the non-verbal messages ... notice how this is familiar or unfamiliar to you ... become aware of what you are experiencing in your body as you remember ... notice any sensations or tension, any physical discomfort ... be an observer of your own experience ... notice your feelings as you recall being there ... and what is happening to your breathing ... notice any fantasies you have about the other person or people and what they are thinking and feeling ... be aware of what you are not saying or doing ... and how you hold yourself back ... notice perhaps what this says about what you need in this situation ... and then breathe a little more deeply ... and turn the searchlight off, returning to the present moment.

Take a few minutes to reflect on that experience – for example, how it felt, how you reacted to different prompts, how easy or difficult it is for you to focus inside yourself – and on what you learned about the process between yourself and the other person/people involved.

What might you either:
- do now to move this situation forward?
- do differently next time you are in a similar situation?

As we have already seen through the case of Jay, head of Park Special School, it is her awareness of process and her authentic way of being and caring for staff and pupils that makes a significant difference to school climate. Her school is a haven of safety and a trustworthy environment for staff and students despite adverse pressures in the wider field. All staff feel they are engaged in co-creating the field and take responsibility for embodying the values of the school. The resulting consistency and care offers vulnerable young people a secure base and opens the possibility for reparative and restorative relationships with dependable adults. For children at risk such attachments are hard to forge or to trust but they are the prime lever for personal change, growth (Atwool, 2006; Batmanghelidjh, 2006) and learning.

Endnotes

[1] Thanks to Pat Thomson, Kerry Vincent and Richard Toalster for agreeing to the use of CATE data in this book.
[2] When staff know they matter pupils are more likely to feel they matter too.

8   *Caring for self and others*

Introduction

At 7.55am on a Monday morning there was a serious accident involving the Champion Secondary School bus. The bus swerved to avoid two cyclists seriously injuring four pedestrians and killing a fourteen year old cyclist instantly. Everyone was in shock. The head teacher, Glynn, was first on the scene and spent the rest of the day and most of the week dealing with the aftermath.

In the hours immediately following the accident he accompanied a police officer to the homes of the deceased child's parents to offer his condolences. He quickly briefed staff, promised he would bring the whole school together at some point that morning and created a space in school for the other passengers to congregate, communicate and console one another with pastoral support from the assistant principal. He then tried to locate the school's educational psychologist and arranged to 'borrow' counsellors from neighbouring county schools.

At 11.30am he called the rest of the school together for an assembly to make sure that everyone was aware of what was happening and give an update on the injured. By that time another child had died of head injuries. He formally announced that the curriculum would remain suspended for the rest of the day and designated this time to tutor groups. He informed pupils that counsellors would be on hand in school all week and, although they would have to prioritise the injured, the counsellors would be available for anyone who wanted some one-to-one time. He also suggested that each tutor group create something together to represent their collective feelings and thoughts on the tragedy and that these would form the basis of a whole school assembly later in the week. He emphasised the need to be sensitive to the feelings of other group members, for whom these untimely deaths might be particularly traumatic and/or bring up painful memories of other losses.

At lunch time Glynn praised staff for being so flexible and responsive and encouraged them to share any feelings and concerns of their own. He also suggested they pool together their ideas for leading the afternoon session. Glynn told staff that they would use the staff meeting planned for the following evening to review the emotional climate and develop a longer term strategy for mourning, whilst also keeping a semblance of normality in delivering the curriculum. The rest of Glynn's day involved writing a letter to parents and taking part in a series of emergency meetings with the chair of governors, the bus company, the LA and of course, the press. Everyone that met him was impressed and reassured by his calmness, warmth and clear thinking.

As he drove home from school later that day, Glynn was overtaken by a driver travelling at high speed who then had to brake suddenly and push his way into the space in front of Glynn's car, almost causing an accident. When they reached the next set of lights Glynn wound down his window and screamed at the man to watch his speed, telling him that he could have killed someone. The man shouted abuse back at Glynn, put two fingers up and speeded off. Glynn started shaking all over and stalled his car. As he tried to turn the ignition key he found himself sobbing behind the wheel, unable to focus on the road or drive anywhere. Eventually, he got the car started and pulled over. He phoned his wife asking her to come in a taxi and drive him home.

That night Glynn had the first of a series of intrusive dreams in which he relived key moments from early that morning, particularly the sound of screeching brakes and the moment of impact on the railings, the smell of rubber on the tarmac and the sight of body parts underneath the bus, the remains of the bicycle and the injured children being escorted or lifted into ambulances. He woke up in a sweat and his heart was racing.

Glynn's chief concern was to support his staff and pupils to the best of his abilities and knowledge. Fortunately, he had learned from a course he had recently attended how important it is to create spaces for people to talk and process their feelings as soon as possible after a traumatic event and thereby reduce the risk of posttraumatic stress symptoms developing. He had swiftly put in place time, space and opportunities for this to happen right across the school. Unfortunately for Glynn, he had decided to skip the final part of the trauma training day. He felt he had far more important things to do 'back at the ranch' than to attend a session called 'The emotional impact of leading in a crisis'. Glynn had grown up in Glasgow and felt he had developed enough resilience to cope with anything life threw at him. His habitual coping strategies involved keeping his emotions out of awareness and focusing his energies on meeting everyone else's needs. On this occasion however, Glynn had underestimated the emotional impact of this trauma on his own health and well being. By leaving early that afternoon he had sold himself short and left himself vulnerable to posttraumatic stress. Unless Glynn is willing to experience and process his own feelings, and accept emotional support from others these early warning symptoms of posttraumatic stress could become chronic and seriously affect his mental and physical health and his capacity for leadership.

The importance of self care

The incident at Champion School is fictional and thankfully not part and parcel of every leader's experience. This chapter will outline the case for emotional self care and offer some simple and effective strategies for putting this in place both during the school day and outside the school environment. It will also highlight some of the personal and professional costs of neglecting the emotional self in an educational climate in which staff and pupils make high emotional demands of their leaders in order to manage their anxiety, insecurity and distress. Emotional self-care is therefore inextricably linked with caring for others and evolving strategies for mutual care.

The majority of the leaders and teacher leaders interviewed for this study found the concept of emotional self-care problematic and viewed it, as Glynn did, as conflicting with their sense of moral purpose and their desire to make a difference to young people in their care. This was especially evident in schools facing extremely challenging circumstances, where many staff felt they had no right to engage in any 'emotional self-indulgence'. In this, they seemed to reflect a societal attitude of disdain towards emotional expression. Reactions, such as those of Glynn in his car, are not considered to be in keeping with a rational, sane adult. Indeed, such unwelcome, irrational intrusions or outbursts are presented as problems to be 'controlled' and 'managed' if good judgement is to prevail. The traditional view of a teacher or leader is of someone able to transcend their emotions in order to keep a level head as John, deputy head of a large comprehensive school, put it:

I think it's really important to keep my emotions separate from the kids … sometimes they are goading you, you know … like they want a response … and I think to myself, 'well, matey, you're not going to get one, you're not going to see what I'm feeling'. I won't give them that satisfaction … it's the old rule isn't it … if you give them an inch they'll take a mile so I have to keep them tight.

Tight? Do you mean you have to keep them out?

Well others might not agree but that's how it's always been for me … that's how I was trained …

So how do you feel about the MEAZ's focus on emotional intelligence then?

Well [head] and I disagree about this and maybe it's a man thing but I want these kids to learn and achieve their best. Many of them have been through the mill and go home to very little of anything each day. I want them to do better. I don't think me showing my emotions would help them. To be quite honest I think it's the last thing they need.

I am hearing that you do feel a lot and that you choose not to show that.

That's right, yes. Some of these kids do make me feel sad and hopeless at times – especially the most disadvantaged ones, the ones with everything stacked against them from the beginning. Life's unfair and they didn't ask to be born, that's what I think.

So you keep these feelings locked away all day?

Mmm.

That sounds quite stressful to me. What happens when you leave school each day? Do you keep them down then?

I don't know, I've never really thought about it. I have been known to shout and scream at other drivers in the car on the way home sometimes – I don't know what other people must think! I go for a run a couple of times a week when I get in – both of those help, I suppose. I just manage most of the time. (S–D–I)

It is easy to empathise with John's position. His apparent lack of care and emotional distance from pupils masks a loving commitment to enhance their life chances through educational achievement. Many of the children and young people in the schools I visited expressed appreciation for teachers, such as John, who are 'safe', meaning able to contain the emotional range of expression in a classroom without shouting, shaming or humiliating pupils. In most cases pupils associated this capacity to respond appropriately with professional competence. In the following extract, Sunil, a year 8 pupil links emotional competence with 'good teaching':

> Ms X … is cool … her lessons are fun … we do lots of different things so we can all be good at something, that's what Miss says, and we help each other … yer look forward to her classes so no-one plays up. If someone does get out of order she's good about it, she can handle it.

> *What's her secret then? What does she do that you like?*

> Well, it depends like … with A, he's in trouble a lot in lots of classes and yesterday he started to kick off … and Miss was cool. … She asked him if he'd do her a favour and sort some stuff out for her at break time … 'cos he's good at that kind of thing and he does like her – and he likes that and so he calms down. Then we gets on with our work. (S-P–FG)

Noddings (1984: 14) describes caring as a 'displacement of interest from my own reality to the reality of another'. By focusing on the 'other' and drawing on an ideal image of self as 'caring', the individual is able to make a decision to act in a caring way. For John, keeping his emotions to himself is an act of care and respect in itself, a recognition that the young people he cares for should not have to care for him. However, it appears that John's perception is limited by a negative construct of his emotional life in relationship with young people.[1] It is the conscious decision to ignore one's personal needs and act on behalf of the 'other' that Noddings defines as 'ethical caring'. Glynn is a model of Noddings 'caring', where 'engrossment' in the other is unhampered by emotional distractions. As one teacher leader said:

> I think it's just a personal feeling I think that's in you, I think you are driven to do it, caring is just part of your personal pride in your job isn't it really? Do it well and do well by them, what else is there? (I–TL–FG)

Similarly, Collins' (2001) research indicates that 'great' leaders channel their ego needs away from themselves towards the larger good of building a great organisation. However, the leaders in his study inhabit the extremes of emotional life. They are for example, modest and wilful, humble and fearless. Movement along a continuum between both polarities makes emotional and physiological demands on the individual. Caring for others often involves some emotional cost to the self, whether that is in the form of intrusive thoughts, disturbed sleep or feeling emotionally drained. The emotional impact of caring can be compounded by the leader's own experience of powerlessness when faced with issues that are beyond their control. The majority of teachers and leaders in this study are motivated by a desire to 'make a difference' and when their strenuous efforts are thwarted by bureaucracy or the apathy of others, or by abject social and economic circumstances, it can be difficult to summon the energy to keep going and resist the gravitational pull of depression and despair, of feeling a failure. When an individual's physical and emotional resources are depleted through exposure to multiple stressors, then their capacity to ride such emotionally challenging phases is seriously diminished and they are more susceptible to stress, to mental health problems and to burnout (Sternberg, 2001: 118). Burnout is defined by Maslach and Jackson as: 'a syndrome of emotional exhaustion and cynicism that occurs among individuals who do "people-work"' (1981: 99). Sternberg suggests physical and psychological burnout diminishes a person's ability to mount an appropriate stress response and ultimately has negative effects on the body's hormonal balance and immune system. Whereas individuals may be quite open about problems with their physical health, people would often rather soldier on than discuss any underlying emotional distress with others. Emotional self-expression is still associated with either 'weakness' or 'bad behaviour' in schools, rather than with authenticity and well being.

It is argued that the emotional demands of working with pupils have become greater since the introduction of the National Curriculum (Watkins, 1999) and many teachers in Cooper's (2004) study of empathy and caring in the teaching profession report feeling less able to care for pupils despite knowing and believing that this is important work. She talks of teachers exhausting themselves trying to make time for needy pupils. Leaders in this study report similar feelings of exhaustion in relation to colleagues, parents and governors:

It's all go ... everyone comes to me and expects me to wave a magic wand and make them feel better or resolve any problems or issues they cannot cope with. It is hard to know where to draw the line

between being responsive and passing responsibility back to them
… sometimes I just want to scream 'what about me?' which is not
right I know. I want to be supportive of staff but I would go under
if I didn't pass some things back to them. (S–H–I)

Recent statistics on teacher stress and head teacher stress, and the
inability to fill head teacher vacancies in England and Wales suggests
that the issue of teacher and leader stress and burnout needs to be
acknowledged and faced by teachers and leaders themselves as well as
by government and local authorities.

Glynn and John, for example, both need to recognise that sustaining leadership practice, in whatever shape or form, involves a duty of
care towards the self. This is not easy when much of the seminal literature on educational leadership foregrounds principles (Senge, 1990),
moral purpose (Fullan, 2001; Collins, 2001), relationships (Pellicer,
2003; Fielding, 2006) and community building (Wenger et al., 2002). It
is important therefore to set these priorities alongside other literature
which addresses the neglect of self in leadership and recognises self
caring as a key pre-requisite for ethical practice and for being effective
in the interpersonal and community focused aspects of the role (Senge
et al., 2005; Covey, 1992; Scott Peck, 1995). Caring for self, otherwise
known as 'self-love' (Scott Peck, 1985), 'sharpening the saw' (Covey,
1992) and 'connectedness' (Sergiovanni, 1992; Senge et al., 2005), is
within the gift of the leader. A choice needs to be made between treating oneself as a thing, an 'It', and thereby colluding with a reductive,
rationalist approach to education, in which the task is super-ordinate to
the person, or treating oneself as a person of worth and value, a 'Thou'.
Aligning self with Thou involves prizing self as a precious resource that
needs to be nurtured and maintained in good spirits and health to
sustain effectiveness over time.

A recent survey of teachers' workload (STRB, 2005) found that on
average head teachers in secondary schools work more than 62 hours
per week and their deputy and assistant heads more than 58 hours,
which represents an increase of two and four hours respectively on the
year before. Interestingly, the survey found that head teachers are perceived as reluctant to create space and time for themselves. It is almost
as if an 'I–It' relationship to self is prized as part and parcel of being a
caring and supportive leader. Such care and support, however, does not
extend to the self. Similarly, Ofsted reported in December 2005 that
despite doing a good job implementing the reductions in administra-

tive tasks and cover for teachers, secondary heads are less good at applying the workforce reform agenda to themselves:

> Few headteachers have considered changes to their workload to take account of the time that should be dedicated to leading and managing a school. The vast majority work long hours during the week and at weekends and accept a heavy workload as part of the job. They report a high level of job satisfaction from working with their staff and pupils and are reluctant to change their established patterns of working. Consequently, they do not see the relevance of the remodelling agenda to themselves. Indeed, the workload of some headteachers has increased. In primary and special schools, they have taken on additional responsibilities such as coordinating curriculum subjects or doing additional teaching in order to release time for their teachers for PPA and cover. In secondary schools, some headteachers continue to be involved in time consuming operational matters particularly in managing behaviour. (Ofsted, 2005a: 10)

This is in evidence in the statements of MEAZ primary and secondary leaders. For example:

> I think they're some of the stresses of being a head, just trying to put it right all the time and sometimes you get it wrong and its like the plates spinning all the time and you drop one. Same thing with trying to put it right for staff. You're letting them develop but you're not putting too much stress on them that they can't do their job effectively. (I–H–I)

> … if people are say organising which children you are having, then I would expect that I would take more than my fair share of the difficult ones. (P–D–FG)

> … part of my philosophy is that I wouldn't expect other people to do things that I wouldn't be prepared to do myself. (S–D–FG)

Certainly concerns about the time-consuming nature of administration and paperwork were cited by most of the leaders and teacher leaders in this study. Self caring is relegated to the bottom of the 'to do' list. A newly qualified teacher states the problem clearly from her perspective:

I think it has become very difficult to sustain yourself and I think a lot of teachers and head teachers have decided that after a number of years they really can't do it any more. (J–J–FG)

Whilst some of this may be related to the leader's internal working model of leadership, to values, to work addiction, to competing demands from family and/or unmet identity needs (such as being visible, indispensable, in control or a rescuer), it is also possible that some leaders have not thought of themselves as a 'Thou' and therefore not taken stock of what they might need by way of emotional sustenance. An 'I–Thou' approach to relationship is a respectful and caring way of being with others, rather than a more objectifying attitude which may involve domination, control or manipulation in order to achieve specific objectives. The 'I–Thou' stance is one in which the self and the other are held in mutual regard and therefore involves a duty of care towards the self. It is as important to listen intently to one's inner experience as to the experience of another person. The Chinese verb for 'to listen' is made up of four characters, which highlight the complexities involved in truly listening to another. They are:

- ears

- eyes

- heart

- undivided attention.

This form of listening is emphasised in counselling training and is essential for the communication of authenticity, positive regard and empathy. It is a way of being with another that honours their uniqueness and their need for human connectedness. Teachers and pupils value leaders who are able to listen in this way and offer such 'I–Thou' relating consistently. Why is it then that so many counsellors, leaders and teachers find it challenging to offer themselves the same undivided attention, to be loving towards themselves, to observe changes in their moods and physiology, to listen to themselves? What could be more important in a profession in which stress and burnout are having a deleterious effect on the future of the profession as well as on schools and individuals? Far from being self indulgent, listening to self is essential maintenance work and ensures that the individual is emotionally fit for purpose. Pellicer equates this kind of listening with the development of self trust:

We don't become leaders until we can trust ourselves enough to listen to our inner voices and know for certain that those voices will guides us in making decisions that are instinctively right for us as leaders. (2003: 182)

Effective leaders take their own emotional, physical, spiritual and intellectual needs most seriously. They acknowledge the intricate relationship between their emotions and physical well being and therefore view emotional and physical self-care as two sides of the same coin. It was Hippocrates (circa 460–370 BC) who maintained that in order to cure the human body it is necessary to have knowledge of the emotions, the mind and the spirit, the whole human system. The purpose of the following exercise is to help you reflect on your physical and emotional health.

Exercise

How good are you at taking care of your emotional self? Place yourself on a scale from 1 (hopeless) to 10 (excellent) in each of the following:

My workspace is comfortable and comforting.

1 — — — — — — — — — — — — — — — — — — — 10

I take regular suppleness/flexibility exercise (e.g. yoga, pilates, body balance). 1 — — — — — — — — — — — — — — — — — 10

I eat healthily most of the time.

1 — — — — — — — — — — — — — — — — — — — 10

I drink lots of water and alcohol in moderation.

1 — — — — — — — — — — — — — — — — — — 10

I acknowledge my strengths and reward myself for work well done.

1 — — — — — — — — — — — — — — — — — — 10

I make time to see people whose company I enjoy.

1 — — — — — — — — — — — — — — — — — — 10

I put aside quality time for my nearest and dearest.

1 — — — — — — — — — — — — — — — — — — 10

I play and laugh a lot. 1 — — — — — — — — — — — — 10

I indulge myself in comforting activities, habits, places.

1 — — — — — — — — — — — — — — — — — — 10

I express my righteous indignation through social action, protests, letters, marches. 1 — — — — — — — — — — — — — — — 10

I show my appreciation of others.

1 — — — — — — — — — — — — — — — — — — 10

I connect with nature, whether the windowsill, garden, parks or countryside. 1 — — — — — — — — — — — — — — — 10

I treat myself regularly.

1 — — — — — — — — — — — — — — — — — — 10

I am able to cry for myself and for others.

1 — — — — — — — — — — — — — — — — — — 10

Review your list. Are there some areas that are more difficult to reflect on and be honest about than others? Just allow yourself to dwell on each one and become aware of your feelings. Accept that this is where you are now. Don't foreclose on your experience or jump to goal setting, just reflect on the quality of your life right now without judgement, guilt or shame. Remember the paradoxical theory of change!

As part of my own development as a teacher, leader and psychotherapist it was necessary to learn that self care routines are most effective when integrated into daily life and not just saved up for days off and holidays. There is a need for adequate time for nourishment, rest, exercise, hobbies, relationships with humans and animals, fun and love. Each person has to find his or her own way of working through their stress and using stressful experiences as transformational processes that enable growth. Whatever methods work for the individual are the 'right' ways, providing they make healthy and appropriate choices. The next section identifies ways in which leaders can practice emotional self-care both within the workplace and beyond. The first of these is enhancing awareness of feelings and needs.

Feelings and needs

According to popular definitions of 'emotional intelligence', Glynn can be seen to be doing a good job as an emotionally intelligent leader. He demonstrates excellent *social skills, stress management skills* and *management* or *control* of his emotions at work (Goleman, 1995; Bar-On, 2000; Stein and Book, 2000), all of which are severely tested in a crisis such as that facing his school community. A growing body of evidence indicates that emotional intelligence, conceived of as these three clusters of behaviours and skills, is positively associated with work performance (for example Slaski, 2001) and with enhanced psycho-physiological coping under stress, as measured by lower blood pressure and lower levels of cortisol in the blood stream (Salovey et al., 2002). However, a study undertaken by Donaldson-feilder and Bond (2004) indicates that the very act of controlling or regulating emotions diminishes mental well being, performance and job satisfaction. By contrast, a willingness and capacity to experience emotions, as opposed to disavowing or repressing them, can be healing.

Previous chapters highlighted the importance of awareness as a means of connecting with the present moment, listening to the emotional self, developing creativity and understanding experience. Examples were used to illustrate how even a brief focus on awareness can contribute to self care and self soothing in times of stress. A combination of deepening the breath and focusing on the present moment are highly effective ways of giving the nervous system a break from the low level persistent stresses of leadership.

Exercise

What stops you from taking a two minute centring break two or three times a day?

What is it that cannot wait for two minutes?

What is more important than your health?

Try it now:

Sit down, make sure your back is well supported by the back of the chair and that your legs and arms are uncrossed, feet planted firmly on the floor. Roll your shoulders back and down and place your hands, palms facing up, on your thighs. Now close your eyes and take ten slow, deep, rhythmic breaths. … With each one breathe a little deeper, starting with the chest, the ribs and then the abdomen … notice the gentle swelling of the chest, ribs and abdomen as you breathe in and the deflation as you exhale … accept any passing thoughts and let them go … after three or four deeper abdominal breaths, work your way back up through the ribs and into the shallower breath in the chest before opening your eyes and returning to normal breathing. Notice how you feel.

Practice this two or three times a day, at least once during working hours.

Attending to and deepening the breath is a simple and effective way of activating the parasympathetic nervous system to counteract the negative effects of stress induced chemicals in the body, such as adrenaline, which have been released from the limbic (emotional) brain. It may be worth pausing here to explain this relationship in more detail. The limbic brain is directly connected to the heart via the autonomic nervous system (ANS). In times of stress the limbic brain is activated and releases hormones to the heart via the ANS. The effect is to increase heart rate, alter blood pressure and put the body under stress. In normal circumstances this chemical process will be interrupted by the parasympathetic nervous system as the limbic brain releases acetycholine to counteract the stress, regulate blood pressure and induce a state of calm or relaxation. However, in situations of continual stress or trauma the system can break down and the heart stops responding to the call of the parasympathetic system to slow down and relax. This process adversely affects the functioning of the immune system. Emotional distress and physical symptoms are therefore calls for action from the heart *and* the brain. Exercises such as meditation, yoga and t'ai chi are all based on the power of the breath to still the mind and restore balance in the body.

Six of the OCTET schools organised whole school INSET days (four of these away from the school environment) to support staff well being. Two of these included optional yoga and breathing classes. In one school staff found this so beneficial that a series of weekly sessions were arranged to give staff the opportunity to experience a range of body balancing classes:

> The school has really taken the idea of nurturing its staff and pupils on board. We pride ourselves on having created a supportive and friendly place to learn and teach. We have run an entire teacher day devoted solely to staff sanity, state of mind and happiness, and offer a range of activities to help staff address the life/work balance. Staff can take part in holistic activities such as chi kung and pilates or for the more energetic, there are regular sports activities for staff and pupils. ... Pupils are provided with counselling, support, mentoring, anger management classes and peer mentoring to help them through stress and support them emotionally. (SIG Poster presentation)

All SIGs reported that attending to staff well being had made a substantial difference to the atmosphere in the staff room and to school climate, as staff took their own experience and learning about well being back into their classrooms. Enhanced communication, collegiality and good humour were reported as outcomes by all six schools, as reflected in the following comment by one SIG member:

> I'll admit I was a bit anxious at first. Although I'd enjoyed our emotional literacy sessions on the OCTET training and recognised that they had made a difference to how I felt about myself, about our role and about each other, I couldn't see many of our staff buying into it ... and I couldn't see how to scale it up until (another SIG) told us what they planned to do and we thought 'yes, we could do that ... we could take staff away for a day's fun and relaxation to rebuild staff morale and well being'. [Our head] was supportive and got it straight away, so with his help and a little injection of cash we planned a day. We all did activities in the morning like we'd done with you on the OCTET days and we had a lot of fun ... and then people chose different taster things to do in the afternoon, like yoga and meditation ... and when the evaluations came in everyone was enthusiastic and appreciative of us as a SIG for organising things ... People said how it had made them feel better and you could feel the difference in school afterwards ... people were lighter and kinder to one another and they smiled more. So we've decided to do a little bit of this regularly as part of our programme of staff well being activities ... and we're doing yoga classes once a week now and then we'll do something else so we don't lose momentum ... and we're sure it will benefit the kids ... well it is already, having happier teachers ... it's like you don't know what you need sometimes until you get it ... and somehow it helped staff to realise that they need looking after too ... so I'm glad we took the risk. (S–TL–I)

Awareness of one's needs can help to clarify feelings and enhance the possibility of completing the cycle of experience. It is the experience of connection (with self and other), satisfaction and withdrawal that counterbalances any negative effects of unfinished business, or environmental distress which are outside of personal control but which exert a negative influence on one's sense of self. As one head teacher said:

> There's just so much going on in this community. The kids come into school having experienced god knows what since they left the day before, anything from emotional abuse to gun crime ... and

they need us to be there for them and not frightened, helpless or judgemental ... I think if you recognise your own feelings, then maybe you can start to develop strategies for coping with yourself and for being more available to listen to their distress and hear their need for care and understanding. (S–H–I)

Exercise

When was the last time you focused on well being as an explicit dimension of your school or classroom environment? Was your focus on adults, pupils or both?

What stops you from attending to staff well being, apart from workload pressures?

How would you feel doing the following?

- Begin your next lesson or team/staff meeting with a fun activity related to the theme or issue you wish to explore.
- Tell your class or team/staff something funny that happened to you recently and encourage them to do the same (in pairs or as a group).
- Finish a lesson with a five minute game or guided imagery to reward/relax the group or finish a meeting with a round of interpersonal learning or appreciation of things individuals have done to support one another.
- Say something nice to everyone in your class/team during a meeting/lesson ... be casual about it ... notice the difference.
- Smile at everyone you meet on a particular day and address as many as you can by name, or just by a friendly 'hello'.

Notice what happens and how you feel? What do you need to feel more comfortable doing any of these?

Creating time and space

Creating time and space represents a real challenge to most leaders and teachers in the hustle and bustle of daily life and yet without opportunities to step back and reflect, both during the working day and outside, school leaders may do themselves a disservice. Self caring is essentially an attitude that does not get switched on and off like a light bulb. It involves a deep commitment to maintain oneself in good psychological and physical health and permeates all aspects of one's life.

In the 1970's Hendricks and Hendricks advocated 'time off well' as one approach to renewal but few leaders nowadays would consider that to be defensible on moral or ethical grounds. One head however, did acknowledge that there are specific times when it is important to cut some slack and put oneself first. Anita, head of a suburban secondary school, describes one such occasion:

> I have to make sure that I am fit to do the job. I put in way over and above what is really acceptable, especially for my family, so I am careful to make sure that I take time for myself and for them. ... Last weekend was the first anniversary of my sister's death. I left work at lunch time and drove down south to my parents ... I knew I needed to be with my mum and my brothers and that I wouldn't do any useful work that afternoon. I'd have felt resentful, and if I'd left at 4pm as I would have been stuck on the M5 for hours and arrived too exhausted and angry to enjoy being there. As it was, I was able to engage and do what I needed to do, and when I came back on Monday morning I did a brilliant assembly, if I do say so myself!

Can you say a little bit more about that?

> Well, I was in touch with my experience from the weekend and how I had felt in the chapel and the words just came. I couldn't have done it without taking that time off for me and my family. It was very healing and I felt as if a weight had lifted when I came back. For the first time in my years of service I didn't feel guilty ... I don't even feel bad about telling you, so that has to be progress! Before M [sister] died I used to take myself and my family for granted but not any more! I would have worried about whether the place would fall apart without me and now I know that's rubbish – life goes on whether I'm here or not. I left J, my deputy in charge on Friday afternoon and he did a grand job ... he seemed proud of himself for having survived. He's been anxious about taking more responsibility – now he knows the world doesn't cave in when I'm not here too ... and I know he'll be really good and grow in confidence if I hand over responsibility in bite-sized chunks for a while. He doesn't know how good he is yet and I remember feeling just like that when I first became a deputy ... I know he'll grow into it, just as I did ... it just takes a bit of time, and a bit of faith from others, that's all ... (S–H–I)

Anita is 'connected' (Senge et al., 2005) with her self and with the common good. She has no desire to make herself indispensable and is committed to developing leadership capacity not just within her senior management team but also in her staff and her students. By attending an important family reunion Anita was caring for herself and her family and nurturing leadership competence in her deputy. In respecting her own emotional needs Anita is also able to honour his. She seems to know instinctively that her relationship with herself models good practice for others. In the accounts of Anna (Chapter 4), Lisa (Chapter 5) and Jay (Chapter 7) it was evident that the capacity to tune into oneself, to own one's shadow and/or to allow creative solutions to seemingly intractable problems are all intimately connected with emotional availability and understanding of others, which Senge et al. (2005) term 'presence'. They assert that the primary asset of any leader is the self and therefore caring for the self becomes an ethical imperative.

Anna asserts that real self care is not possible without adequate quality time for herself. For her, the long summer break is a time for processing the year and minimising the risk of repeating any errors of judgement. The long break is therefore a time for deeper learning, letting go of the past and preparing oneself for new beginnings:

> My first two years have been so rewarding and I am proud of what we have achieved. I needed the summer holiday to think over the past year ... to reflect and integrate what we have done and to let it all settle inside. I had a difficult incident with a member of staff on the last day of term – it was really unpleasant and I was left carrying a lot of distress ... it took a few weeks to move myself into a position where I could let go of that and find a way of re-engaging with her after the summer ... We all need a fresh start in the Autumn ... the children and the staff ... It's important not to carry things forward and save them up to cash in at a later date ... much better to let things go and move on. I don't know if she has been able to reach the same place towards me ... I hope by offering her an amnesty she will reciprocate and we can leave all that behind. If it weren't for the long break I don't think I would have survived my first two years. ... The job takes so much out of me that I know I can't sustain it for very long, I'll have to move onto something else. (M–H–I)

Jay actually did leave her school and take up a role in the local authority. She was sadly missed by her staff but, having suffered a traumatic personal bereavement, she felt the time was ready to give something back to herself ...

> My partner died just before Christmas after a long illness and I only took a few days off work. The staff were fantastic and the past two terms have been good ... we've really reaped the public rewards for all our hard work ... but I need some time for me now and to decide what I want to do with the rest of my life. ... I have taken a secondment and will do some work within the LA which means I will be able to support the school in a different way and hopefully influence the LA's policy on inclusion. (SS–H–I)

Jay is able to walk away from her school because of the ethos of care, mutuality and shared leadership that she has developed.

> The staff are amazing and there is enough leadership in the school to sustain it through my absence. I do trust my deputy to run the school well and other staff deserve the chance to move into new leadership positions and spread their wings ... it's important they take their own authority. They give a lot of credit to me and don't take enough for themselves ... so I hope I'm doing the right thing for me, for them and for the school. (SS–H–I)

Once more, putting the self first in awareness and in a spirit of deep commitment to the school can be seen as facilitative of leadership development in colleagues. It is an attitude of trust and empathic attunement to the needs of others to grow and develop as people and as professionals and honours the self actualising tendency discussed in Chapter Five.

A great deal of stress results from fear of change and a sense of powerlessness (Seligman, 1975) and therefore creating space to explore such feelings is an important dimension in the alleviation of stress. It is imperative that staff do not feel emotionally abandoned as they take on more leadership roles and responsibilities. In one school, staff bemoaned the absence of care from their head. However, in the discussion it emerged that this absence had contributed to more collegial forms of care and support:

> one of the biggest things here is that when something happens that's good, we say to each other 'I really enjoyed your assembly',

'I really liked your painting', 'hasn't so and so's writing come on? I had him last year and I can see how he's improved', and I think that sort of thing supports us because we always tell each other. We go around the school finding good practice and we tell each other. (J–J–FG)

The literature on school leadership tends to overlook the need for specific spaces in which individuals and groups can express their feelings, experience acceptance and empathy and grow through their anxieties, hurts and mistakes. The focus group discussions were viewed in themselves to be in some way restorative and helpful. Counsellors have regular individual or group supervision to process the feelings that are generated through their work with vulnerable people, to review the appropriateness of their interventions and to consider alternative ways of supporting their client's process. Supervision provides a means of simultaneously caring for self and others. Three MEAZ heads highlighted the key role of one-to-one coaching relationships in helping them to reflect, review and plan their work with individuals, groups, the whole school and external agencies. For example, Anita says:

The coaching has definitely worked. Now I automatically think 'don't jump in, don't be on the defensive and send their emotional levels even higher'. Yes I think it has quite an amazing effect on me that I feel more able to cope. That when there's an angry parent there I don't sort of say to [my secretary] 'leave the door open, hang about, they might get violent' because I'm pretty certain I can deal with it now. (I–H–I)

They also recognised the value of this for colleagues:

There's a kind of coaching that's needed for staff to enable them to take the initiative, live with the consequences and take responsibility. (S–H–I)

The issue of creating space is also closely allied with trust building and with collegiality. In one IQEA school a SIG group member described the importance of a safe space, a place of belonging and mutual trust through which strategic discussions and sensitive issues can be discussed openly and honestly:

We have a good staff at X school and generally speaking we get on very well with one another but the Cadre Group members seem to have a very close relationship with each other especially when we are actually sitting in the meetings. We can actually say things that we know need to be talked through and we know full well that they will not go outside ... It was unwritten at the beginning and then somebody said something like 'I am going to say something now and I don't want it to go outside these walls' and we all agreed and even at that point we all realised that there was a lot of trust and confidentiality ... and we used the discussions about individuals and departments to think about how best to involve and mobilise them ... so it wasn't gossiping, it was always about how to do the people work to help move the school forward ... (S–TL/SIG–I)

By contrast a new member of staff in a MEAZ school expressed her dismay at the lack of a safe space where staff could meet, a situation that had arisen due to a culture of workaholism:

I must admit when I came in one thing that shocked me the most was that there was nobody hardly ... and it's got better actually since I've been here, over the year, but nobody came to the staffroom, I found that amazing that people didn't come into the staffroom ... I was shocked by it. I was thinking, 'what are they doing? why don't they just sit and relax for a while?', I was think-ing, 'god, is this expected of me, can I not have my lunch? (P–TL–FG)

This particular teacher leader demonstrated her leadership skills and met her own needs. She organised a series of special lunchtime events to tempt her new colleagues back into the staffroom. Staff acknowl-edged that the main purpose of the staffroom space up until that point had been to meet staff candidates on interview days and hold weekly staff meetings or grab a cup of coffee at break times.

Young people too need spaces in school in which to relax and enjoy one another's company. The vast majority of the photos taken by young people to describe positive feelings focused on two interrelated aspects of school life, namely relationships with peers and teachers and also play spaces beyond the school buildings, where pupils could relax and spend time together socially. Jay's special school and Lisa's primary school were notable exceptions. At Sidegate School, for example, it is pupils' spaces, in the shape of individual desks, lockers and the school hall that feature most strongly in their photos:

> And I took one of the children playing with the basketballs in the hall because I felt that, that's kind of the things that we play in the school and it helps us relax when we go into class. (Rhys, year 5)

> I took this photo of the lockers because it makes me feel as though I can keep my belongings very safe for the rest of the day when I come into school. (Claire, year 6)

Projects such as 'A Quiet Place' in Liverpool (Spalding, 2000) and 'School as Sanctuary' in Chicago (Antrop-Gonzalez, 2006) provide potent evidence of the value of safe spaces in schools for marginalised and vulnerable young people. These provide models of good practice involving interdisciplinary teams and demonstrate significant benefits for individual pupils and corresponding advantages for their mainstream classrooms and school climate. Such spaces are equally important for the less vulnerable as they struggle with the social and emotional tasks of growing up in a challenging and turbulent world. The following chapter will explore the prevalence of posttraumatic stress in schools and consider the implications of this for the emotional work of school leaders.

Endnote

[1] I have regretted not checking out with John whether he would also choose to withhold positive emotions from young people.

9 *In trauma and in health*

Be kind, for everyone you meet is fighting a hard battle.

Plato

Introduction

Increasing concerns about behaviour and violence in schools put leaders under pressure to find effective ways of controlling the most challenging pupils in order to minimise the negative effects of their behaviour on teaching and learning and school climate. Fearful of events spiralling out of control, teachers' and leaders' efforts to 'manage' such pupils unwittingly compound their underlying problems. Behaviour management may actually exacerbate behaviour problems in schools by creating greater distance between adults and young people whose primary deficit, and hence greatest need in life, is for love, care and proximity to a protective, safe adult. Recent evidence from neuroscience and from studies of therapeutic work with children 'at risk' and young offenders, indicate that posttraumatic stress is a significant cause of social, emotional and behavioural difficulties, including violence. Camilla Batmanghelidjh's work with the most traumatised and behaviourally challenging young people has led her to conclude:

> The truth is that very disturbed children take a very long time to provide visible outcomes. Their outcomes are personal, and their successes are often individual and emotional first, before they become visible in the world of academia and work ... the truth is that before an educational outcome there needs to be an emotional one. (2006: 22–3)

This chapter offers a brief introduction to the causes and consequences of posttraumatic stress in young people and identifies the emotional conditions needed to support colleagues and pupils, enhance wellbeing and cooperation and promote learning throughout the school.

Traumatic stress and brain development

Perls (1942:179) maintains that *'The awareness of and the ability to endure, unwanted emotions are the condition sine qua non for a successful cure.'* Although talking from his experience of the therapeutic context, Perls' assertion has been supported by research into the human brain, which indicates that well being is related to the capacity to experience the full range of emotions. However, some people are better able to tolerate and experience negative emotions than others. The roots of this tolerance may of course have some genetic component. However, in the majority of cases, it is the level of exposure to trauma in childhood and the capacity of caregivers to respond appropriately and soothe the distressed child that will shape the emotional brain's capacity to tolerate difficult emotions. It is important at this stage to offer a brief insight into brain development and into what constitutes trauma in childhood in order to promote more in-depth understanding of the emotional self and of that self-in-relationship with challenging colleagues and young people.

At birth the baby's brain is unfinished and can be compared to a new PC in its box, waiting to be wired up by a competent technician. The development of the brainstem, which is fundamental to the healthy development of the rest of the brain, is formed between birth and eight months of age. Attachment theorists argue that humans are 'wired' to seek the protection of significant others, particularly in times of danger. The human baby (and young child) will do everything in their power to maintain that closeness and feel safe. They will cry, howl, kick and so on until they feel the presence and responsiveness of caregivers. Normally, this leads to the physical and emotional relaxation of tension. In this way intimate attachment bonds shape a child's sense of safety and self worth and provide the blueprint for future relationships and behaviours. If the baby does not receive enough attention or emotional *attunement* from loving caregivers the pathways that regulate their physiological states and form the foundations for later self-soothing remain undeveloped. Brain scans of Romanian orphans for example, show a black hole where the social and emotional centres of the brain should be (Schore, 1994).

Between years one and two the midbrain, which organises sensory stimuli and regulates motor activity, develops alongside the limbic system, the emotional centre of the brain. This is where basic emotional states are experienced, which the concurrent/subsequent development of language and humour in the upper brain (neo-cortex) help to mediate. This upper brain provides a protective layer around the emotional brain and also houses the capacity for abstract reasoning, for musical and artistic abilities and for more complex emotional processing (Sunderland 2004).

The 'competent technician' that helps to hardwire the brain listens to the baby and young child, 'tuning into' their emotional needs and meets the intensity of their experience with physical and emotional comfort, with cuddles, soothing words, stroking, caring facial expression and loving eye contact. This soothing activates relaxing opioids in the brain and anti-anxiety chemicals such as GABA.[1] In this way the baby, and later the child, is helped to manage overwhelming feelings of sadness, anger and fear (Damasio, 1994) and learns to *balance* their body, emotions and states of mind. Eventually, feeling safe, emotionally understood and cared for within their environment, they internalise this experience and learn to soothe themselves. In this way there is *coherence* between the child's internal sense of integration and their external sense of connectedness (attachment) with others (Siegel and Hartzell, 2003). They also develop greater resilience to later traumatisation (Schore, 1996).

Repeated exposure to stressful situations in which the child is not met with comfort or soothing can hardwire the brain and body for over-responsiveness to even the slightest stressor. The primitive survival mechanisms of fight or flight are evident in their behaviours, whether withdrawal, isolation, disruption or violence. Taking the analogy of a central heating system, it is as if the pump will not heed the 'off' setting on the programmer and continues to work full pelt even when it is not needed. In such cases the body is flooded with catecholamine hormones, such as cortisol and adrenalin, which raise blood sugars, heart rate and blood pressure, thereby compromising the body's immune system. This is evident in the defensiveness and alert behaviour of some adults and many children and young people in schools and makes the emotional work of leading, teaching and learning such a challenging experience for all.

Young people and adults who have experienced 'good enough' parenting in the early years but who have suffered subsequent traumas (such as war, natural disaster, migration, accident, abuse) and losses (such as separation, death, divorce, transition) may present with similar emotional and behavioural problems. If the underlying hardwiring in the emotional brain is in place, however, then the chances of healing enough to engage with life and learning are greater.

In my view a key emotional task of leadership is the activation of calming opioids and GABA in the school environment. This can do much to alleviate some of the low level anxiety experienced by colleagues and pupils and create a climate in which insecurely attached young people feel some measure of safety. Even a small gesture, such as being smiled at and called by name, can make a significant difference to an individual's sense of safety and belonging. From a process perspective such emotional leadership sets the tone whereby soothing, relaxing relationships are more the norm than the exception:

> For good or ill as a leader, leaders cast a shadow. What kind of shadow do we cast? How we behave and conduct ourself will have a massive effect on the culture of the organization. If we moan they will moan, if we get cross they will think it okay to get cross, if we look too busy to listen then they will look too busy to listen, if we cut them off they will cut others off, if we look in a panic they are more likely to look in a panic. If we inspire they will inspire, if we coach others they will coach others, if we show respect and high expectations, they will do also, if we demonstrate emotional intelligence and kindness, they will develop that too. (Munby, 2006)

Lisa, one of the EAZ head teachers had been impacted by the relationship between brain development and learning, which she had discovered at a University of the First Age conference workshop.

> We wanted to get the children to their optimum level for learning at all times. And I learned that unless you've got, it's quite simple really, the best ideas are often simple, unless you have relaxed and happy learners then the part of the brain that controls you is the flight part of the brain and therefore the children are battling against trying to manage their emotions and that interferes with the children's intellectual development. So we made a conscious effort not to shout at kids and to help them feel at home at school, from the smell of warm toast when they come through the door in the morning and get breakfast in the dining room, to giving them control over some of the conditions for learning ... we installed a filtered water dispenser and they can go and get water any time they feel dehydrated or need to stretch their legs ... and on the whole they don't abuse it ... Some of my colleagues thought I was

mad to do this in this neighbourhood but I want children to leave the school with a tool kit for how to learn ... Most of them, they haven't got all the middle class external ways of support ... and children will never learn how to learn and they will never be able to manage their own learning unless they make that big step forward out of the comfort zone and take the risk ... That's my vision. It's hard though. It's a hard one and we have to make it safe enough first for them to trust themselves. (P–H–I)

Lisa's intentions are clearly understood and appreciated by pupils in years five and six whose choice of photos included the water fountain, which most of them valued as supportive and calming. Rhys for example, says:

I took one of the water ... the water fountain we have, and we have this so it relaxes – relax yourself and it helps us work and that's it, cool water, we have a little bit and it helps us relax. (P–P–FG)

Similarly, Carrie identifies a self-directed learning opportunity as enhancing her self belief as a learner:

I took one of the touch typing lesson what we learn on the computers, so you can put your hands on it, you do not ... you don't look down on the computer, you just look up at the telly and type like grown-ups do ... so it makes you feel good about yourself and you know you can do something well if you practice long enough and so you know you can learn anything. (P–P–FG)

Unbeknown to Lisa, the strategies she has developed are valuable in counterbalancing some of the effects of trauma and neglect, whether caused by government, community or parents. Her recognition of the importance of safety is evidenced in the attachments between her pupils and their form teachers, which is made possible by a rolling tutor programme where, as far as possible, pupils stay with one tutor for at least two years. It is likely that the safety and security of being with a dependable adult on a daily basis plays a significant part in enabling pupils to engage with the opportunities on offer.

Certainly for severely traumatised young people who have learned to survive in emotional isolation, a secure attachment to a tutor can make a significant difference. It is the absence of such relationships that leads many to exclude themselves from secondary education (Wetz, 2006). A secure attachment relationship can only be formed with severely traumatised young people if the adults are willing to commit themselves to the young person over time. This involves demonstrating care and respect consistently, being firm and forgiving about relapses into difficult behaviours (Harris, Vincent et al., 2006) and being available for contact when needed.[2] In other words teachers need to walk the extra mile with such young people to help them feel safe enough in school to keep them there. This commitment is akin to that of a marriage contract 'for better or worse, in sickness and in health'. Without such commitment the repeated induction by the child to abandon them and repeat their previous experience will be intense. Some of the neglect and abuse suffered by these young people is so far beyond the 'normal' range that, in the absence of direct experience of a person's home situation, it can be difficult to sustain empathy over the long term, especially when their behaviour escalates.

Most adults have experienced some traumas even at the hands of loving parents. As discussed earlier, even 'normal' parenting practices in this culture, such as leaving a baby to cry, shouting at a toddler and smacking a young child hard all have an hormonal cost.[3] Teicher's research (2000) demonstrates that regular shouting damages the corpus callosum, the main information highway that links the left and right hemispheres of the brain and enables the different characteristics of the brain, such as mathematical, logical, rational and visual, kinaesthetic, emotional to communicate and work synergistically with one another for effective communication and learning (Gazzaniga, 1972). Margot Sunderland maintains that 87% of adults in the UK shout at children regularly and that one in five parents think it is fine to smack a toddler. It would be interesting to know how much shouting children and young people experience in classrooms on a daily basis. Set this against Sunderland's claim that it is not necessary to frighten a child very much to establish a fearful response to the environment and to the world, it is likely that our schools are full of adults and children whose brains have been hardwired for overactive fear.[4] This is the emotional brain's legacy from isolation, uncomforted distress and unmourned grief.

Self care and other care are therefore interrelated and are most likely to be effective if emotional well being, which 'stimulates the capacity for learning, creativity and human exchange' (Orbach, 1999) is written into the fabric of school life.

Exercise

Reflect on your own experience as a child ... and as an adult now ...

Close your eyes and call to mind an experience of being terrified as a young child. Relive the experience as vividly as you can – notice what is happening in your body as you remember – notice the intensity of your feelings – and be aware of what support is available to you – who is there and how do they respond ... what validation of your emotions do you receive ... is there any emotional containment? ... if so, how do you experience this? – what is happening in your body now as you remember? – now leave that memory behind and fast forward to your life now – recall a recent experience of feeling fearful and relive that as fully as you can ... notice the intensity of your feelings and be aware of what you do to keep yourself safe – and to feel better – notice also who you turn to for support as an adult – and how they respond – what is it you need in future to help you when you experience a situation in which you are afraid? ...

Reflect on the relationship between your adult self and your child self. What was missing, if anything, when you were younger and how do you ensure your emotional needs are met in times of stress and difficulty?

Guerra's (2003) extensive study of school-based violence and violence prevention methods in the United States, leads her to the conclusion that deficits in the social and emotional development of some young people are key contributors to aggressive and even extreme violent behaviour. Certainly, the capacity for empathy is severely impaired by violence, in which no subsequent tenderness is offered to soothe the child. Being either the victim or perpetrator of terror is the only way they can contact their feelings. Furthermore, their emotional numbness leaves them cut off from potential sources of comfort as adults and peers avoid being in contact with them and reinforce their felt sense of worthlessness and isolation. Batmanghelidjh's long-term involvement with vulnerable young people in London accords with this view:

> The urban child warrior, like the religious terrorist, is a new brand of soldier. Their will to die comes from the same space. They have nothing to live for, they are exhausted with living, feelingless, numb and emotionally cold. The urban child soldier, the terrorist, the child who kills, they are all the same children of murdered childhoods ... The murder of childhood is killing us all. (2006: 11)

Maintaining punitive, disciplinary measures to end aggression and violence therefore merely serves to perpetuate the 'drama triangle' (Karpman, 1968) and does little to resolve the causes of distress in the perpetrator. There is nothing that can be done in the school environment that would frighten such children into behaving more appropriately. By contrast, schools that are based on secure relationships between adults and children, and that actively promote a 'culture of wellness', are highly effective in supporting the social and emotional development of those who are prone to aggression and challenging behaviour (Guerra, 2003) as well as those suffering from other forms of traumatic stress.

Posttraumatic stress

Shapiro (1995) coined the term 'small-t' traumas to describe those universal experiences that are part and parcel of living in hierarchical systems and affect most people at different points in their lives. These include humiliation, shaming, aggression, abuse, unexpected loss, bereavement and so on. Efforts to manage the emotional impact of 'small-t' traumas using reason and logic have, however, failed to diminish the emotional intensity or influence of these original wounds. As Servan-Schreiber says:

> Undoubtedly, we have thought about it quite a bit on our own, received a lot of advice from friends and family, read magazine articles about this type of situation and how to respond to it, perhaps even read self-help books. From all these sources, we learned, often very well, how to *think* about the situation, and we know how we *should* be feeling about it. However, this is often where things are left: with feelings that have lagged behind and remain anchored in the past even after our rational (cognitive) understanding has changed. (2004: 81–2)

As repetitive change injuries and incidents of school violence become increasingly common and space to process such events is squeezed out by the demands of the curriculum, it is likely that many teachers and pupils experience 'small-t' traumas in school more often than they would like. Such 'small-t' traumas induce some degree of fear which may manifest as imperfection, neediness, failure, emptiness, loss of identity and so on. Awareness of the cumulative effect of small traumas on experiencing is an important aspect of self care that is often overlooked. If, for example, failure at some task at school during childhood had led a teacher to humiliate, peers to bully and parents to punish an individual harshly, then it is likely that the emotional imprint in the brain will be activated by the very prospect of failure and send the adult into a state of terror. If they had learned to dissociate from their feelings as a child they may not connect their emotional responses to new situations with earlier life events and therefore feel ashamed of feeling so intensely! If they are able to remember, then they may relive the original events in their dreams or, when triggered by other stressors, in the present moment, including the same physiological changes and incapacity for speech they had experienced as a child. All the sounds, smells, tastes, physical sensations, emotions and thoughts associated with the original event can re-evoke core beliefs about self, such as 'I am hopeless, I am useless, I am a failure'. Such self beliefs are often precursors of anxiety, depression, eating disorders, substance abuse and other self-harming practices, such as alcoholism, workaholism and so on. For other victims of big 't' violence or trauma, terror is sublimated by acting out, taking power and using violence or intimidation to terrorise others.

At times of collectively experienced trauma, such as those experienced by Glynn and his school community in the previous chapter, everyone is likely to be emotionally affected. For those directly involved in the accident there is a real chance of posttraumatic stress reactions. Even though Glynn's foresight and good planning has minimised the risk of this, some staff and pupils, including Glynn himself, may experience flashbacks, for no apparent reason at all, as if they were reliving the experience over again. Scans of peoples' brains following a traumatic event show that, if the experience has not been talked about and processed during the first 24 hours, then it is as if the trauma leaves an imprint, or scar on the brain, just as untended cuts or burns leave scars on the skin. This scarring can be seen in the form of an overactive amygdala, the fear centre of the emotional brain, an active visual cortex, the photographic centre of the brain and an underactive left prefrontal cortex, the area of the brain responsible for language. Therefore, individuals suffering from posttraumatic stress experience flashbacks, intense feelings of terror and are unable to find words to express what is happening. The emotional brain and the rational, thinking brain cannot communicate about this incident and therefore the individual is stuck in an emotional drama they cannot control. Having bypassed awareness of his own emotions and thoughts on the day of the accident, Glynn is a prime candidate for such a posttraumatic stress reaction unless he processes his feelings when he gets home and receives tender loving care from his wife and family.

An emerging body of evidence suggests that many young people who present in school with emotional and behavioural difficulties are actually suffering from post traumatic stress disorder (Pynoos et al., 1995; Salloum et al., 2001), and, unable to tolerate or name their emotions, they are easily triggered into a 'fight or flight' response either acting out their distress in anti-social behaviour or turning their aggression back on themselves through self-harming practices, such as cutting, substance abusing and so on. Ovaert and colleagues (2003) discovered that a reduction in posttraumatic stress disorder symptoms is positively associated with a reduction in the incidence of aggressive or disruptive behaviour. Ofsted (2005c) supports this view and suggests that schools which focus on behaviour management and pay insufficient attention to emotional health and well being may actually provoke or intensify patterns of misbehaviour in young people.

One of the EAZ teacher leaders highlighted how much effort needs to be taken to talk traumatised young people through each day. He spoke of the emotional and physical demands made of him in his previous school to create classroom conditions in which young vulnerable children could engage in learning:

> At [infants school] I spent all day long talking 20 odd children through the day and by 2.45 I was exhausted talking those children through the day. It's not the teaching that tires, its getting the children through the day. When you have got such a high percentage of special needs, children with emotional difficulties, behaviour problems etc., and you know that some of them have little emotional support outside school, you try and make it okay for them to relax and settle down ... and that's without any of the planning or anything ... all that is on top. (I–TL–FG)

If we return to the cycle of awareness then it possible to understand all the different forms and degrees of posttraumatic stress as a process, in which the individual oscillates between (overwhelming) sensation and mobilisation (freeze, fight or flight) and by-passes the awareness stage of the cycle. In physiological terms, this means that the parasympathetic nervous system is not triggered to release soothing opioids and counteract the hormonal flooding of the brain and body by the sympathetic nervous system. In the case just cited it is the teacher's persistence in 'talking children through the day' that contains their anxiety and enables them to engage in some learning.

Claire, a pupil at Sidegate Primary School, describes how a fishtank in the school foyer helps her to move into a more relaxed frame of mind:

> I took this picture of the goldfish tank because it makes me feel as though I am very relaxed and calm and ready to learn as soon as I see it. (Claire, year 6)

This is echoed by pupils at Redington Infants School, where a large tropical fishtank is located in the pupils' reading area and pupils expressed how they felt personally attached to the fish, which are credited with human powers:

How do you feel when you come into school each day?

Happy?

What makes you happy?

The fish swimming in the tank ... they make you feel good and excited.

Excited?

Yeh, cos you know you can spend some time with them every day when you do quiet reading ...

What's that?

Well ... you choose a book, any book you want to read and you can sit on a cushion by the fishtank and read it ... and ...

Yeh, if you get stuck you can ask the fish to help you cos they are clever.

Yeh, they do help yer remember the words. (I–P–FG)

Inducing calm and developing awareness are both important ways of breaking the pattern of traumatic stress responses, supporting the individual to move round the gestalt cycle towards completion. Two strategies are offered here to support this process with young people in school settings: guided imagery and fighting with love. However, it must be noted that using these techniques are only advisable with this group when there is a secure attachment between teacher and pupil and therefore enough trust to risk feeling.

Guided imagery

The first step in raising awareness of feelings is learning to tune into self. Whereas most adults can close their eyes, focus on their breathing and stay with their inner experiencing at least for a minute or two, this can be very challenging for some young people. It is therefore necessary to develop a range of strategies for fitting such work into the mainstream curriculum. Hendricks and Wills (1975) have devised a number of awareness activities for children and adults to relax the body and mind and thereby induce a sense of calm and soothing. Stevens (1971) and Oaklander (1988), both gestalt therapists, devised a number of awareness exercises to facilitate greater awareness and understanding of self and I have adapted many of these for use with leaders, teachers and pupils in classroom settings. Of particular relevance here are fantasy journeys or guided imagery work, which have applications across the curriculum and which children, young people and adults of all ages find relaxing and emotionally centring. As a teacher leader in a secondary school I found these particularly helpful in calming a class after break times, and especially after lunch on a Friday afternoon! Despite initially resisting the exercises by fidgeting, giggling or being negative, for example, pupils overcame their embarrassment and looked forward to their little trips into unknown territory where they could use the power of their imagination to summon up feelings of safety, connectedness, relaxation or joy. Perhaps one of the simplest ways of using guided imagery is to start the day by visualising it unfold positively and benignly for all. From a field theory perspective starting out positively can influence how one copes with the day and how one contributes to the larger field. Positive thinking can be a key element in self care and there is even evidence of improved responses to influenza vaccinations in 'positive thinkers' (Vedhara et al., 1999).

Hall et al. (1990) have developed a range of scripted fantasies for use in classroom settings. One classic script is particularly valuable for young people who are vulnerable, unprotected or suffering the effects of traumatic events and can be found in a range of resources for professionals working in this area. In essence, pupils use their imaginations to create a 'safe place' which they can draw on at will as an escape from overwhelming feelings or difficult situations, therefore helping to develop their own emotional resources and building self support. Teachers and leaders need their own 'safe place' and therefore this exercise is reproduced here. It is a powerful and non-threatening way of calming and soothing the self. However, it does presume that the individual or class is familiar with breathing exercises as a way of settling down as well as the kind of awareness exercises presented in earlier chapters.

Exercise

Take a couple of deep breaths and allow your body to settle down and relax ... take your time ... and when you are ready ... think about some of the things that are making you feel anxious, angry, or hurt in your life right now ... perhaps they are keeping you awake at night or stop you from concentrating on your work ... you do not have to tell anyone what they are ... that is your choice ... just notice what comes up and notice how you are feeling as you remember. ... Now ... in your imagination paint a picture of somewhere you can go and feel safe ... where no one can hurt you ... or upset you ... just allow a picture to form in your mind's eye ... it might be somewhere you know or it might be somewhere that would make you feel much better and much calmer ... imagine yourself in this safe place. ... Take a good look round ... what does it look like? ... what does it sound like? ... does it have a smell? ... What are you doing? ... and how are you feeling right now in this safe place? ... enjoy the feeling of safety ... no one can spoil this special place ... it is all yours to come back to whenever you feel anxious, angry, upset or hurt ... all you have to do is take yourself there inside your head. ... Hold onto your feelings as you gently come back into the room ...

(Adapted from Hall et al., 1990)

This scripted fantasy can be an invaluable asset for anyone suffering from emotional distress or who is susceptible to overwhelming feelings of fear and anxiety. For the most traumatised young people, its success is dependent on a high degree of safety in the classroom and the willingness of a teacher to stay alongside them if they become distressed:

There is no doubt that the use of scripted fantasy in the classroom will generate a range of feeling states in the students. They may become quiet and reflective, they may become sad or even cry, they may become excited or energised. It is the acceptance of the feelings of sadness, hurt, grief and even despair that some teachers have difficulty in handling in themselves and their students or their students. ... If you are shocked by the expression of feelings in others, particularly students, then the use of scripted fantasy is not for you. Certainly there is no evidence to show that the expression of feelings is bad for the students. If anything, the opposite is the case and the sharing of feelings enables students and teachers to come together as a more cohesive and caring group. (Hall et al., 1990: 17)

As we have seen in Chapter Four, when pupils were given thoughts and feelings books and regular opportunities to share the contents with other classmates, their grasp of emotional vocabulary was impressive, their conversations an important source of emotional support and this work was highly compatible with mainstream oracy work. Scripted fantasy can be a powerful way of adding to and enriching such classroom experience and have the added benefit of making learning enjoyable and relaxing. The following comments are indicative of classroom impact reports presented by teachers involved in the Promoting Emotional Development project run by colleagues at the Centre for the Study of Human Relations in four families of schools across a large Midlands city:

I have recently been trying the scripted fantasies with my class as a form of relaxation. At first the children found this to be quite a strange experience as they had never come across this type of activity before, but after a few tries at this over the weeks they are familiar with it and they are taking it more seriously. The discussions afterwards about what they saw in their fantasies were amazing – some really imaginative things were coming out and the children really enjoyed this. I have tried it a few times when they needed settling down and also on Fridays at the end of the day after long hard work.

All pupils expressed a wish to do the exercise again. Pupils were eager to share comments about what the exercise had meant to them. Writing included a high proportion of feeling words, including advanced vocabulary.

The activity was extremely successful. The children thoroughly enjoyed the new experience. One or two of the children couldn't close their eyes. They would do it for a couple of seconds and then open them again. This was fine and I did not object – even though their eyes were open they were still joining in with the activity. (CSHR, 2003: 15)

Participation in experiential learning courses in human relations (Hall et al., 1988) and emotional development (CSHR, 2003; Harris and Biddulph, 2000) can help teachers develop the awareness, confidence and competence to offer disturbed young people attuned, emotionally reparative relationships as well as to use more creative strategies for enhancing pupil awareness, developing an emotional vocabulary and sharing their experiences in a group. Eighty-two per cent of the teachers involved in the Promoting Emotional Development Project stated that they felt more confident in their ability to use imagery to develop student self awareness following participation in the programme (CSHR, 2003).

Fighting with love

Barratt (2006) asserts that it is the repression of personal aggressiveness that places society at risk of violence. He cites the World Council of Churches' view of a socially ambivalent relationship to violence, in which it is experienced as both repelling and attractive, alarming and entertaining, destructive and protective. He also claims that the Western world is living in a 'cultural state of trauma', which robs individuals of their quality of life. Barratt coins the phrase 'fighting with love' and stresses the importance of helping children to learn to fight well, a psychological task he ranks alongside learning to love. Gandhi, Martin Luther King and Nelson Mandela may well epitomise fighting with love but they had the benefit of life experience and a searching intellect to guide them. When working with young people in schools it is important to help them find ways of fighting well that do not rely solely on the capacity for verbal debate and social skills. Guided imagery is one way of developing an internal 'caretaker self' (Kalsched, 1996), that protects the self from harm. Martial arts training and boxing are more physical ways of learning to defend the vulnerable, trauma-tised self. In both these sports, the fighter lowers their centre of gravity to give themselves more stability, flexibility and power. The very act of dropping the centre of gravity calms the self and the other, and Barratt cites an occasion when he assumed this stance as he turned to face a group of youths, one of whom had just stolen his wallet. In taking up this more centred posture he felt safer in himself and was able to calmly ask the offender to return his wallet. Surprisingly, he did so without question.

A punch or kick delivered from this centred place strikes an energetic balance between fighting and self-protecting. Physical Education classes that teach 'fighting well' could work to support those with inner trauma and build their confidence whilst team sports help to develop their social skills (Bailey, 2006). In my own classes I was not aware or skilled enough to teach young people to fight well in these ways. However, I did instinctively realise that some adolescents could not cope with their anxiety and were constantly on the edge of acting out their feelings in aggressive ways. I therefore kept a corner of the classroom as a 'chill out zone' and stocked it with a range of resources for pupils to access at will including paper, paints and a pile of used yellow pages and retail catalogues which pupils could rip to shreds to get rid of surplus energy and aggression. A dustpan and brush was also provided so that they could clean up the mess afterwards! Charmaine, who lived in care and found many of her relationships in school difficult to manage, established a routine whereby she would spend the first ten minutes of every lunchtime session either painting furiously or using all her strength to destroy a glossy brochure before she went for lunch. I would make sure I was in the room and just spent that time sorting out my desk and preparing for my afternoon lessons. It felt important that Charmaine had a witness and someone to make a connection with, although we often said nothing. Years later when she was approaching 20 years of age she found my university e-mail address through Google and sent me a simple message:

> I don't know if you remember me but I remember you. Thank you for helping me. I missed you when you left. PS I still tear up books when I'm angry.

From this I understood that Charmaine had found an effective way to support her vulnerable self as an adolescent in and out of school. Giving young people the tools to support themselves emotionally and socially is a gift for life as well as a respectful way of responding to adolescents who eschew relationships with adults until they have proved themselves trustworthy and 'safe'.

Promoting well being and good health therefore involves creating opportunities for hormone levels in staff, children and young people to return to normal and the organism to be 'at rest' (Sternberg, 2001). The prevalence of emotional distress and trauma in schools places a particularly challenging duty of care on leaders and teachers to create environments in which adults and pupils feel safe and trusting enough of their environment to relax their hypervigilance and give their bodies a chance to recover. Given the 'shaking' in society discussed in Chapter Two there is a pressing need for time and space for such emotional work for all members of the school community. Moreover it is essential for those members whose capacity to engage constructively with people and with learning has been disrupted by events beyond their control.

The implementation of the Children Act 2004 and the New Service Framework for Children holds much promise for traumatised, vulnerable young people in that they will legitimise dialogues about pastoral issues between teachers and other professionals which are meant to hold children's interests at heart. Moreover, young people may have a key worker with whom they can form a secure attachment relationship ands who can help them bridge the cultural gap between their experiences in and out of school. However, there is some concern that pastoral care may be subjected to a version of standardised testing with accountability based purely on measurable behavioural outcomes and all that implies for the quality of helping relationship with young people, or for their engagement in negotiating what matters most to them. Also, unless the concept of Every Child Matters is extended to include Every Teacher Matters, it is likely that schools with the highest proportion of vulnerable children will be least well positioned and resourced to offer the high levels of support, care and love traumatised young people need and deserve to transcend their difficulties, engage with learning and gain some measure of hope.

Endnotes

[1] GABA is also found in alcohol and chocolate, which is part of the reason for our addictions! It can be activated via certain drugs and is used to treat anxiety and mood disorders.

[2] See Toni's story in Harris and Biddulph, 2000.

3 It is important to note that psychological pain and physical pain are located in the same part of the brain.
4 To substantiate this assertion Sunderland cites research in which rats that are frightened for one second each day develop a permanent state of fearfulness by day ten.

Postscript

When I first thought about this book my primary intention was to raise awareness of the emotional dimensions of school leadership and leadership practice. My central aim was to offer leaders at all levels in schools some of my understandings and insights into the emotional work of school life. This is not easy territory. The basic premise of this book is that leadership is primarily concerned with relationships in schools. These are messy, complex, frustrating but ultimately rewarding when they are nurtured and developed.

My central treatise in this book is that emotional experience lies at the heart of school leadership and that the most effective leaders work at this level principally intuitively and fundamentally. It is very clear and probably self evident, that school leaders, teachers and pupils are all in powerful relationships within the school and therefore to one another. Whether we acknowledge it or not, there is a high degree of interconnectedness and interdependence. The important thing to remember is that leaders can choose to build a trusting climate where these relationships can work most positively at classroom and school level or they can undermine or even destroy them. My question to you is how do you as a leader create the conditions for relationship building and trust within your classroom, subject area or school?

The ways in which leaders evoke and respond to emotions are of paramount importance. If you are angry, they are angry. If you are pessimistic, they will be pessimistic. But if you are enthusiastic, positive and upbeat, their emotional response will be influenced by yours. On a daily basis you model the leadership you expect and get. You shape the expectations, frustrations and ambitions of others. School leaders have a significant role to play in modelling relationships based on human caring and respect and in facilitating personal, as well as academic development. So what leadership do you model in your role?

This book is about human relationships. It is intrinsically about what leadership is, what leaders do. You as a leader can choose everyday to dismiss someone or recognise them. You can only do this because you are in a relationship with the people you lead, whether you like them or not. Your emotional responses make a difference.

In this book I have argued that:

- Rational models of leadership simply 'cannot hold' in the 21st century school. Educational change places high demands for personal change. New ways of leading are needed that acknowledge leadership as primarily an emotional and not a rational activity.

- A new model of leadership is needed that addresses the emotional awareness and congruence of leaders much more closely.

- Effective leaders pay attention to their inner growth and recognise that they must fully develop themselves as human beings if they are to develop as leaders. Leaders are attuned to their own feelings and able to emotionally attune to others.

- Learning about leadership will require developing awareness of one's vulnerabilities, one's capacity to wound and how one's own behaviour might affect the emotional experience of others.

- Leadership is essentially about leadership practices not leadership tasks. Developing understanding of interpersonal processes is fundamental if leaders are to foster emotional awareness and literacy in others and engage community members in the co-creative process of learning and school improvement.

- Leadership is a social, moral and ethical process which is fundamentally about raising individual self esteem and collective response-ability, and facilitating leadership development at all levels.

- Leaders recognise that every member of the school community feels vulnerable at times and that this emotional fragility can be expressed in ways that isolate and distance the individual from others and hence from potential sources of care and support. Leaders therefore create a climate in which emotions can be safely discharged without fear of escalation, humiliation or abandonment.

- Leaders recognise the primacy of secure attachment relationships for well being, resilience and learning, particularly for those who have been traumatised and emotionally frozen, whether by an absence of love, by neglect, emotional abuse or physical violence. They make sure their school is a 'secure base' for all.

- Leaders understand their role and responsibility for establishing and reinforcing an upward spiral of emotional experience in school. They recognise that positive emotions lead to positive cognitions, positive behaviours and increased learning capability, which in turn fuel positive emotions and so on.

If we are serious about improvement and change in our schools then leaders are an important, if not the most important, lever to secure improvement and change. Leadership and leaders make a difference for good or ill. If we want to generate the forms of leadership more suited to the 21st century we must pay attention to the emotional dimension of leadership. The old managerialist models of leadership are no longer suited to an age that is fast paced, technologically driven and globally focused. We are using theories and models of leadership that simply do not suit the contemporary educational landscape. We need a human side to leadership and leaders who can engage authentically, both emotionally and intellectually. We need leaders who fundamentally realise the need to engage, interact and connect with others and ultimately to recognise the common, frail and ultimately vulnerable humanity that we all share:

> If they find working with us stimulating and challenging and they feel valued and they respect us and want to work for us and with us then they are more likely to want to become leaders themselves and to have the skills to be good in the role. (Munby, 2006)

References

Ackerman, R.H. and Maslin-Ostrowski, P. (2004) 'The wounded leader and emotional learning in the schoolhouse', *School Leadership and Management*, 24 (3): 311–28.

Alexander, E. and Thomas, D. (2004) 'Values education at Greenfield Lower School: The seamless robe', *Forum*, 46 (2): 59–62.

Allport, G. (1955) *Becoming: Basic considerations for a psychology of personality.* New Haven CT: Yale University Press.

Antrop-Gonzalez, R. (2006) 'Toward the *School as Sanctuary* concept in multicultural urban education: Implications for small high school reform', *Curriculum Inquiry*, 36: 273–301.

Aspy, D.N. and Roebuck, F.N. (1977) *Kids Don't Learn from People They Don't Like.* Amherst, Mass: Human Resource Development Press.

Atwool, N. (2006) 'Attachment and resilience: Implications for children in care', *Child Care in Practice*, 12 (4): 313–50.

Bailey, R. (2006) 'Physical education and sport in schools: A review of benefits and outcomes', *Journal of School Health*, 76 (8): 397–401.

Baldwin, M. (2000) 'Interview with Carl Rogers on the use of self in therapy', in M. Baldwin (ed.), *The Use of Self in Therapy.* New York: Haworth Press.

Barkham, P. (2006) 'Bristle while you work', *The Guardian (G2)*, 3 August. pp. 6–9.

Bar-On and Parker, J.D.A. (2000) *The Handbook of Emotional Intelligence.* San Francisco, CA: Jossey-Bass.

Barratt, J. (2006) 'Fighting with Love', Guest Lecture, BACP Annual Conference, London, 6 October.

Batmanghelidjh, C. (2006) *Shattered Lives.* London: Jessica Kingsley Publishers.

Beatty, B.R. (2000) 'The emotions of educational leadership: Breaking the silence', *International Journal of Leadership in Education*, 3 (4): 331–57.

Beatty, B. and Brew, C. (2004) 'Trusting relationships and emotional epistemologies: A foundational leadership issue', *School Leadership and Management*, 24 (3): 329–56.

Beisser, A. (1970) 'The paradoxical theory of change', in J. Fagan and I.L. Shepherd (eds), *Gestalt Therapy Now*. New York: Harper and Row.

Bennett, N., Wise, C., Woods, P. and Harvey, J.A. (2003) *Distributed Leadership*. Nottingham: National College for School Leadership. www.ncsl.org.uk/index.cfm?pageID=literaturereviews (accessed 14 December 2004).

Bennis, W. (2003) *On Becoming a Leader*. Cambridge, Mass: Perseus Books Group.

Berne, E. (1967) *Games People Play: The psychology of human relationships*. New York: Grove Press.

Biddulph, M. (2006) 'Sexualities equality in schools: Why every lesbian, gay, bisexual or transgender (LGBT) child matters', *Pastoral Care in Education*, 24 (2): 15–21.

Blaney, P.H. (1986) 'Affect and memory: A review', *Psychological Bulletin*, 99: 229–46.

Blasé, Joseph and Blasé, Jo (2003) *Breaking the Silence: Overcoming the Problem of Principal Mistreatment of Teachers*. Corwin Press.

Block, P. (1993) *Stewardship: Choosing Service Over Self-interest*. San Francisco, CA: Berrett-Koehler.

Bowlby, J. (1988). *A Secure Base*. New York: Basic Books.

Buber, M. (1937) *I and Thou*. Edinburgh: T&T Clark.

Bullough, R.V. Jr, Mortensen Bullough, D.A. and Mayes, P.B. (2006) 'Getting in touch: Dreaming, the emotions and the work of teaching', *Teachers and Teaching: Theory and Practice*, 12 (2): 193–208.

Burns, J.M. (1978) *Leadership*. New York. Harper and Rowe.

Burns, J.M. (2003) *Transforming Leadership*. New York: Grove Press.

Caldwell, B. (2004)

Caldwell, B.J. (2006) *Re-Imaging Educational Leadership*. Australian Council for Educational Research, Camberwell, Victoria: Australia.

Capra, F. (2003) *The Hidden Connections: A science for sustainable living*. London: Flamingo.

Carlyle, D. and Woods, P. (2002) *The Emotions of Teacher Stress*. Stoke on Trent: Trentham.

Centre for the Study of Human Relations (CSHR) (2003) *Promoting Emotional Development. Final Evaluation Report*. Nottingham: School of Education.

Choy, A. (1990) 'The winner's triangle', *Transactional Analysis Journal*, 20 (1): 40–6.

Ciarrochi, J. and Scott, G. (2006) 'The link between emotional competence and well-being: A longitudinal study', *British Journal of Guidance and Counselling*, 34 (2): 231–43.

Clarkson, P (1994) *The Achilles Syndrome*. Shaftesbury: Element Books.

Clarkson, P. (2004) *Gestalt Counselling in Action*. London: Sage Publications.

Collins, J. (2001) *Good to Great: Why some companies make the leap … and others don't*. New York: Barnes Noble.

Conti-O'Hare, M. (2002) *The Nurse as Wounded Healer*. Sudbury, MA: Jones & Bartlett Publishers.

Cooper, B. (2004) 'Empathy, interaction and caring: Teachers' roles in a constrained environment', *Pastoral Care*, 22 (3): 12–21.

Covey, S. (1989) *The Seven Habits of Highly Effective People*. London: Simon & Schuster.

Cox, T. (1978) *Stress*. London: Macmillan Press.

Csikszentmihalyi, M. (1993) *The Evolving Self: A Psychology for the New Millennium*. Harper Perennial: New York.

Damasio, A.D. (1994) *Descartes' Error: Emotion, reason, and the human brain*. London: Penguin Books.

Damasio, A.D. (1999) *The Feelings of What Happens: Body, emotion and the making of consciousness*. London: Vintage.

Daniels G. and French S. (2006) *Work-life Balance of Managers, Professionals and Head Teachers. A Report for the NAHT*. www.naht. org.uk/userfiles/416995563/nahtcomparativereport325sept06.pdf (accessed 10 October 2006)

Day, C., Harris, A., Hadfield, M., Tolley, H. and Beresford, J. (2000) *Leading Schools in Times of Change*. Buckingham: Open University Press.

D'Augelli, A.R., Grossman, A.H., Salter, N.P, Vasey, J.J., Starks, M.T. and Sinclair, K.O. (2005) 'Predicting the suicide attempts of lesbian, gay, and bisexual youth', *Suicide and Life-Threatening Behavior*, 35 (6): 646–60.

Dench, G., Gavron, K. and Young, M. (2006) *The New East End*. London: Profile Books.

Department for Education and Skills (DfES) (2003a) *Excellence and Enjoyment*. London: HMSO.

Department for Education and Skills (DfES) (2003b) *Raising Standards and Tackling Workload: A National Agreement*. London: HMSO.

Department for Education and Skills (DfES) (2005) *School Workforce in England: Provisional Teacher Sickness Absence in 2004 and Teacher*

Ethnicity, May *2005 SFR 0/2005*. http://www.dfes.gov.uk/rsgateway/ DB/SFR/s000578/SFR20-2005.pdf (accessed 8 June 2005).

Department for Education and Skills (DfES) (2006) *Permanent and Fixed Period Exclusions from Schools and Exclusion Appeals in England, 2004/05 SGR24/ 2006*. www.dfes.gov.uk/rsgateway/DB/SFR/ s000662/SFR24-2006.pdf. (accessed 9 May 2006).

Department of Health (2004) *Survey of the Mental Health of Children and Young People in Great Britain*. London: HMSO.

Dinham, J. and Scott, C. (1996) *The Teacher 2000 Project: A Study of Teacher Satisfaction, Motivation and Health*. Sydney: University of Western Sydney, Nepean.

Donaldson-Feilder and Bond (2004) 'The relative importance of psychological acceptance and emotional intelligence to workplace well-being', *British Journal of Guidance and Counselling*, 32 (2): 187–203.

Dossey, L. (1982) *Space, Time and Medicine*. Boston, MA: Shambhala Publications.

Dowrick, S. (1992) *Intimacy and Solitude*. London: The Women's Press.

Durrant, J. and Holden, G. (2006) *Teachers Leading Change*. London: Paul Chapman Publishing.

Easen, G. (2006) 'Heads Lobby on Workloads Problem', 20th July. http://news.bbc.co.uk/1/hi/education/5198574.stm (accessed 23 July 2006).

Elmore, R. (2003) *Knowing the Right Thing to Do: School improvement and performance-based accountability*. Harvard: Harvard University Press.

English, H.B. and English, A.C. (1958) *A Comprehensive Dictionary of Psychological and Psychoanalytical Terms*. New York: Longmans Green.

Evans, R. (1996) *The Human Side of School Change*. San Francisco, CA: Jossey Bass.

Evans, R. (2000) 'The Authentic Leader', in *The Jossey Bass Reader of Educational Leadership*. San Francisco, CA: Jossey Bass. pp. 287–308.

Fagan, J. (1970) 'The Tasks of the Therapist', in J. Fagan and I.L. Shepherd (eds), *Gestalt Therapy Now*. New York: Harper & Row.

Fagan, J. and Shepherd, I.L. (eds) (1970) *Gestalt Therapy Now*. New York: Harper & Row.

Fielding, M. (2006) 'Leadership, personalization and high performance schooling: Naming the new totalitarianism', *School Leadership and Management*, 26 (4): 347–70.

Fineman, S. (1993) *Emotion in Organisations*. London: Sage Publications.

on to the special issue', *Journal of Clinical Activities, ts & Handouts in Psychotherapy Practice*, 2 (2): 1–3.

and Wills, R. (1975) *The Centering Book: Awareness activities , parents and teachers*. Englewood Cliffs: Prentice-Hall.

has, J. (2004) 'Passing between the clashing rocks: The est for a common and inclusive identity', *Pastoral Care*, 22 .

A. (1983) *The Managed Heart*. Los Angeles: University of a Press.

C. (1991) *Education Leadership: The moral art*. Alban, NY: iversity of New York Press.

2001) *The Search for a Secure Base*. Hove: Brunner-Routledge.

and Reynolds, D. (2001) 'The past, present and future of improvement: Towards the third age', *British Educational Journal*, 27 (4): 459–75.

and Scally, M. (1981) *Lifeskills Teaching*. London: McGraw-

and Walsh, I. (2005) *Violence and What To Do About It*. n: WAVE Trust.

. (2006) 21st Annual Survey of Senior Staff Appointments in s in England & Wales, www.naht.org.uk/userfiles/ 92293/howsonreportpress.pdf (accessed 18 July 2006).

.A., Duncan, B.L. and Miller, S.D. (1999) *The Heart and Soul of e: What works in therapy*. Washington: APA.

R. (2006) 'All of humanity is here!', *Pastoral Care in Education* 24 (2): 45–9.

Shimotsu, S., Matsumoto, T. and Okada, A. (2006) 'Deliberate arm and childhood hyperactivity in junior high school nts', *European Child & Adolescent Psychiatry*, 15 (3): 172–6.

. (2006) *The Impact of Affluenza on Modern Relationships*. hote Address, BACP Annual Conference, London, 6 October.

.D. (2006) 'Big change question: How do leaders' own lives and r educational contexts, influence their responses to the mmas and tensions they face in their daily work?', *Journal of cational Change*, 7: 99–100.

B. and Woods, P. (1996) 'Feeling de-professionalised: The social struction of teacher emotions during an Ofsted inspection,' mbridge Journal of Education*, 26 (3): 325–43.

n, S.M. (1987) *Humanising the Narcissistic Style*. New York: Norton Company.

Fink, D. (2005) *Leadership for Mortals*. London: Paul Chapman Publishing.

Fouts, G., Callan, M., Piasentin, K. and Lawson, A. (2006) 'Demonizing in children's television cartoons and Disney animated films', *Child Psychiatry and Human Development*, 37 (1): 15–24.

Freire, P. (1995) *Pedagogy of Hope. Reliving Pedagogy of the Oppressed*. New York: Continuum.

Freshwater, D. and Robertson, C. (2002) *Emotions and Needs*. Buckingham: Open University Press.

Freud, S. (1915–17). Lecture twenty one, in *Introductory Lectures on Psychoanalysis* (1955) S. E. 15, 16, ed. and trans. James and Alix Strachey, London: Hogarth Press.

Fullan, M. (1995) 'Emotion and Hope: Constructive concepts for complex times', in M. Fullan (ed.) *The Challenge of School Change*. Arlington Heights: Skylight.

Fullan, M. (2001) *Leading in a Culture of Change*. San Francisco: Jossey-Bass.

Fullan, M. (2006) *Beyond Turnaround Leadership*. Priestly Lecture. University of Birmingham, 24 May 2006.

Gazzaniga, M. (1973) 'The Split Brain in Man', in R. Ornstein (ed.) *The Nature of Human Consciousness*. San Francisco, CA: W.M. Freeman & Co.

Gendlin, E. (1978) *Focusing*. New York: Bantam.

Gentile, J.R. (1996). 'Setbacks in "The advancement of learning"?', *Educational Researcher*, 25 (7): 37–9.

Gerhardt, S. (2004) *Why Love Matters*. Hove: Brunner-Routledge.

Gilligan, S.G. and Bower, G.H. (1984) 'Cognitive consequences of emotional arousal', in C. Izard, J. Kagan and R. Zajonc (eds) *Emotions, Cognitions & Behaviour*. Cambridge: Cambridge University Press. pp. 547–88.

Goldstein, K. (1939) *The Organism: A holistic approach to biology derived from pathological data in man*. New York: American Books.

Goleman, D. (1995) *Emotional Intelligence*. London: Bloomsbury.

Goleman, D. (2000) 'Leadership that gets results', *Harvard Business Review* 7 (2): 78–90.

Gray, J., Hopkins, D., Reynolds, D., Wilcox, B., Farrell, S. and Jesson, D. (1999) *Improving Schools: Performance and potential*. Buckingham: Open University Press.

Green, J.D., Sommerville, R.B., Nystrom, L.E. and Darley, J.M. (2001) 'An fMRI investigation of emotional engagement in moral Judgment', *Science*, 293.

Greenberg, L.S., Rice, L.N. and Elliott, R. (1993) *Facilitating Emotional Change*. New York: Guildford Press.

Greenhalgh, P. (1994) *Emotional Growth and Learning*. London: Routledge.

Greenleaf, R.K. (1977) *Servant Leadership*. New York: Paulist Press.

Guerra, N.G. (2003) 'Preventing school violence by promoting wellness', *Journal of Applied Psychoanalytic Studies*, 5 (2): 139–54.

Guskey, T.R. (1997) 'Evaluating staff development begins by identifying its purpose', *The Developer*, April, p. 3.

Haidt, J. (2001) 'The emotional dog and its rational tail: A social intuitionist approach to moral judgment', *Psychological Review*, 108: 814–34.

Hall, E., Hall, C. and Leech, A. (1990) *Scripted Fantasy for the Classroom*. London: Routledge.

Hall, E., Hall, C. and Sirin, A. (1996) 'Professional and personal development for teachers: The application of learning following a counselling module', *British Journal of Educational Psychology*, 66: 383–98.

Hall, E., Hall, C.A., Harris, B., Hay, D., Biddulph, M. and Duffy, T. (1999) 'An evaluation of the long-term outcomes of small-group work for counsellor development', *British Journal of Guidance and Counselling*, 27 (1): 99–112.

Hall, E., Woodhouse, D.A. and Wooster, A.D. (1988) 'An evaluation of in-service courses in human relations', *British Journal of In-Service Education*, 11 (1): 55–60.

Halton, W. (1995) 'Institutional stress on providers in health and education', *Psychodynamic Counselling*, 1 (2): 187–98.

Hargreaves, A. (1998) 'The emotional politics of teaching and teacher development: With implications for educational leadership', *International Journal of Leadership in Education*, 1 (4): 315–36.

Hargreaves, A. (2000) 'Mixed emotions: Teachers' perceptions of their interactions with students', *Teaching and Teacher Education*, 16: 811–26.

Hargreaves, A. (2001) 'Emotional geographies of teaching', *The Teachers College Record*, 103 (6): 1056–80.

Hargreaves, A. (2004) 'Distinction and disgust: The emotional politics of school failure', *International Journal of Leadership in Education*, 7 (1): 27–41.

Hargreaves, A. and Fink, D. (2003) 'The Seven Principles of Sustainable Leadership', Paper submitted to *Educational Leadership*, December

2003. www2.bc.edu/~hargrea[...] 15 July 2005).

Hargreaves, D. (1995) 'School cul[...] improvement', *School Effectiv[...] 23–46.

Hargreaves, D.H. (2001) 'A capital[...] school improvement', *British [...] 487–503.

Harman, R. (1982) 'Working at the [...] S., (5): 39–48.

Harris, A. (2006) *Distributed Leader[...] Practice?* Keynote lecture presente[...] 17 October.

Harris, A. and Muijs, D. (2005) *In[...] Leadership*. New York: Open Unive[...]

Harris, A., Clarke, P., James, S., Harris[...] *Schools in Difficulty*. London: Conti[...]

Harris, A. and Crispeels, J.H. (eds)[...] *Educational Systems*. Abingdon: Rout[...]

Harris, B. (2001) 'Facing the challenges[...] Kong: An experiential approach to t[...] *Care in Education*, 19 (2): 21–31.

Harris, B. (2003) 'Cultural Issues in Coun[...] and C. Hall (eds) *Counselling P[...] RoutledgeFalmer.

Harris, B. (2004) 'Leading By Heart?', *Schoo[...] 24 (4):

Harris, B. and Biddulph, M. (2000) 'Surviv[...] scale study of the role of group wo[...] teachers' professional practice', *Pastoral[...] 9–16.

Harris, B. and Pattison, S. (2006) 'Counsel[...] Adding value to education for childr[...] *Australian Educational Researcher*, 33 (2): 9[...]

Harris, B., Vincent, K. Thomson, P. and Toalst[...] child know they matter? Pupils' views[...] exclusion', *Pastoral Care in Education*, 24 (2[...]

Hart, S., Dixon, A., Drummond, M.J. and McIn[...] *without Limits*. Maidenhead: Open Universit[...]

Hecker, L.L. and Kottler, J.A. (2002) 'Growi[...]

Introducti[...] *Assignmen[...]

Hendricks, G.[...] *for childre[...]

Henzell-Thor[...] heroic qu[...] (3): 35–4[...]

Hochschild,[...] Californ[...]

Hodgkinson[...] State Un[...]

Holmes, J. ([...]

Hopkins, D[...] school [...] *Research[...]

Hopson, B.[...] Hill.

Hoskin, G[...] Croyd[...]

Howson, J[...] Schoo[...] 10627[...]

Hubble, [...] *Chang[...]

Hudson,[...] 2006[...]

Izutsu, T[...] self-[...] stud[...]

James, [...] Key[...]

Jansen,[...] thei[...] dile[...] *Edu[...]*

Jeffrey,[...] co[...] *Ca[...]*

Johns[...] &[...]

Joyce, B.R. (1982) 'Dynamic Dysequilibrium: The intelligence of growth', *Theory Into Practice*, 23 (1): 26–34.

Joyce, B., Calhoun, E. and Hopkins, D. (2002) *Models of Learning-tools for Teaching*. Milton Keynes: Open University Press.

Jung, C.G. and von Franz, M.L. (1964) *Man and His Symbols*. Garden City New York: Doubleday.

Kabat-Zinn, J (1990) *Full Catastrophe Living: Using the wisdom of your body and mind to face stress, pain, and illness*. New York: Delacorte Press.

Kabat-Zinn, J. (1994) *You Go, There You Are: Mindfulness meditation in everyday life*. New York: Hyperion.

Kalsched, D (1996) *The Inner World of Trauma*. London: Routledge.

Karpman, S. (1968) 'Script drama analysis', *Transactional Analysis*, Bulletin 7 (26): 39–43.

Kasser, T. (2002) *The High Price of Materialism*. Cambridge, MA: MIT Press.

Kellerman, B. (2004) *Bad Leadership*. Cambridge, MA: Harvard Business School Press.

Kington, A. (2006) *The Emotional Context of Teaching: Teacher identity*. Paper presented at BERA Conference, Warwick, 7–9 September.

Kohl, H. (1994) *I Won't Learn from You*. New York: New Press.

Kottler, J.A. and Hecker, L.L. (2002) 'Creativity in therapy: being struck by lightning and guided by thunderstorms', *Journal of Clinical Activities, Assignments & Handouts in Psychotherapy Practice*, 2 (2): 5–21.

Kouzes, J.M. and Posner, B.Z. (2000) 'The Janusian Leader', in S. Chowdbury (ed.) *Management 21C*, Englewood Cliffs, NJ: Prentice Hall.

Kouzes J.M. and Posner, B.Z. (2003) *Encouraging the Heart: A leader's guide to rewarding and recognizing others*. San Francisco, CA: Jossey Bass.

Lambourn, A. (2006) 'Teachers, kicked, bitten, hit and stabbed', *Nottingham Evening Post*, 13 April.

Lasch, R. (2002) 'Top Leadership', *Ivey Business Journal*, May/June: 45–8.

Le Doux, J. (1998) *The Emotional Brain*. London: Orion.

Levin, D. (1981) 'Approaches to Psychotherapy: Freud, Jung and Tibetan Buddhism', in R.S. Valle and R. Ackartsberg (eds) (1993) *The Metaphors of Consciousness*, Plenum: New York. Cited in Rowan, J. (1993) *The Transpersonal, Psychotherapy & Counselling*. London: Routledge.

Lewin, K. (1951) *Field Theory in Social Science*, D. Cartwright (ed.) New York: Harper and Brothers.

Lipman-Blumen, J. (2005) 'Toxic leadership: When grand illusions masquerade as noble visions', *Leader To Leader*, Spring 2005: 29–36.

Liston, D. and Garrison, J. (eds) (2004) *Teaching, Learning and Loving: Reclaiming passion in educational practice.* London, RoutledgeFalmer.

Loader, D. (1997) *The Inner Principal.* London: Falmer Press.

Loder, T.L. and Spillane, J. (2006) 'Big Change Question: How do leaders' own lives and their educational contexts, influence their responses to the dilemmas and tensions they face in their daily work?', *Journal of Educational Change 7:* 91–2.

Lodge, C. (2005) 'From hearing voices to engaging in dialogue: problematising student participation in school improvement', *Journal of Educational Change,* 6: 125–46.

Luft, J. (1984) *Group Processes: An introduction to group dynamics.* California: Mayfield Publishing Company.

Lupton, R. (2005) 'Social justice and school improvement: Improving the quality of schooling in the poorest neighbourhoods', *British Educational Research Journal,* 31 (5): 589–604.

MacBeath, J. (2006) 'Finding a voice, finding self', *Educational Review,* 58 (2): 195–208.

Maslach, C. and Jackson, S.E. (1981) 'The measurement of experienced burnout', *Journal of Occupational Behaviour,* 2: 99–113.

Maslin-Ostrowski, P. and Ackerman, R.H. (2000) 'On being wounded: implications for school leadership', *Journal of Educational Administration,* 38 (3): 1–11.

Maslow, A.H. (1970). *Motivation and Personality* (2nd ed.). New York: Harper and Row.

Maslow, A.H. (1971) *The Farther Reaches of Human Nature.* New York: Viking.

Meltzer, H., Gatward, R., Goodman, R. and Ford, T. (2003) 'Mental health of children and adolescents in Great Britain', *International Review of Psychiatry,* 5 (1–2): 185–7.

Mental Health Foundation (2006) *Truth Hurts, Report of the National Inquiry into Self Harm among Young People.* London: Mental Health Foundation.

Muijs, D. and Reynolds, D. (2001) *Effective Teaching: Evidence and practice.* London: Paul Chapman Publishing.

Munby, S. (2006) *Future Leadership – Future Leaders.* Keynote address. SSAT National Conference, Birmingham, 30 November–1 December.

Myss, C. (1997) *Why People Don't Heal and How They Can.* New York: Three Rivers Press.

NAS/UWT (2004) 'Enough is Enough: NASUWT campaign against violence, abuse and harassment', www.nasuwt.org.uk/templates/internal.asp?nodeid=70334&arc=0 (accessed 3 March 2006).

Nias, J. (1996) 'Thinking about feeling: the emotions in teaching', *Cambridge Journal of Education*, 26 (3): 293–306.

Noddings, N. (1984) *Caring – A Feminine Approach to Ethics and Moral Education*. Berkeley and Los Angeles: University of California Press.

Oaklander, V. (1988) *Windows to Our Children. A Gestalt therapy approach to children and adolescents*, 2nd Edition. New York: Gestalt Journal Press.

Office for National Statistics (ONS) www.statistics.gov.uk/CCI/nugget.asp?ID=1163 (accessed 28 October 2006).

Ofsted (2005a) *Remodelling The School Workforce*. December, Doc No: 2596.

Ofsted (2005b) *Primary National Strategy: An evaluation of its impact in primary schools 2004/2005*. December, Doc No: 2396.

Ofsted (2005c) Healthy Minds, Promoting Emotional Health and Wellbeing in Schools (HM12457). www.Ofsted.gov.uk/publications. Accessed 30 October 2006.

Orbach, S. (1999) *Towards Emotional Literacy*. London: Virago.

Ovaert, LB., Cashel, M.L., Sewell, K.W., McConnell, R.A. and Sim, A.H.J. (2003) 'Structured group therapy for post-traumatic stress disorder in incarcerated male juveniles', *Journal of Orthopsychiatry*, 73 (3): 294–301.

Parks, J. (2000) 'The Dance of Dialogue: Thinking and feeling in education', *Pastoral Care in Education*, 18 (3): 11–15.

Parse, R.R. (1992) *Hope: An international human becoming perspective*. Sudbury, MA: Jones & Bartlett.

Pederson, P, (2000) *Handbook for Developing Multicultural Awareness*, 3rd Edition, Alexandria, VA: ACA.

Pederson, P.B. (1997) *Culture-Centred Counseling Interventions*. Thousand Oaks, CA: Sage Publications.

Pellicer, L.O. (2003) *Caring Enough To Lead*. Thousand Oaks, CA: Corwin Press.

Perls, F.S. (1942) *Ego, Hunger & Aggression*. London: George Allen & Unwin.

Perls, F.S. (1969) *Gestalt Therapy Verbatim*. Toronto: Bantam.

Perls, F.S. (1970) 'Four Lectures', in J. Fagan and I.L. Shepherd (eds) (1970) *Gestalt Therapy Now*. New York: Harper & Row.

Perls, G., Hefferline, R.F. and Goodman, P. (1951) *Gestalt Therapy*.

London: Souvenir Press.

Place2Be (2006) *Annual Report.* London: London: Place2Be.

Polster, E. and Polster, M. (1973) *Gestalt Therapy Integrated.* New York: Random House.

Pynoos, R.S., Steinberg, A.M. and Piacentini, J.C. (1995) 'A developmental model of childhood traumatic stress', in D. Cicchetti and D.J. Cohen (eds) *Developmental Psychopathology: Vol 2. Risk, disorder and adaptation.* New York: John Wiley & Sons.

Renwick, F. and Spalding, B. (2002) 'A Quiet Place project: An evaluation of early therapeutic intervention within mainstream schools', *British Journal of Special Education,* 29 (3):144–9.

Reynolds, D. Harris, A., Clarke, P., Harris, B. and James, S. (2006) 'Challenging the challenged: Developing an improvement programme for schools facing exceptionally challenging circumstances', SESI 17 (4): 1–16.

Rogers, C.R. (1951) *Client-Centred Therapy.* London: Constable.

Rogers, C.R. (1961) *On Becoming A Person.* Boston: Houghton Mifflin.

Rogers, C.R. (1968) 'Some thoughts regarding the current presuppositions of the behavioural sciences', in W. Coulson and C.R. Rogers (eds) (1968) *Man and the Science of Man.* Columbus, OH: Charles E. Merrill. Reprinted in H. Kirschenbaum and V. Land Henderson (eds) (1990) *The Carl Rogers Reader.* Boston: Houghton Mifflin. pp. 263–78.

Rogers, C.R. (1980) *A Way of Being.* Boston: Houghton Mifflin.

Rogers, C.R. (1992) 'The necessary and sufficient conditions of therapeutic personality change', *Journal of Consulting and Clinical Psychology,* 60 (6): 827–32.

Rosenthal, H. (2002) 'Samuel T. Gladding on Creativity', *Journal of Clinical Activities, Assignments and Handouts in Psychotherapy Practice,* 2 (2): 23–33.

Rutter, M., Giller, H. and Hagell, A. (1998) *Antisocial Behaviour by Young People.* Cambridge: Cambridge University Press.

Salloum, A., Avery, L. and McClain, R.P. (2001) 'Group psychotherapy for adolescent survivors of homicide victims', *Journal of the American Academy of Child and Adolescent Psychiatry,* 40 (11): 1261–7.

Salovey P., Stroud, L., Woolery A. and Epel, E.S. (2002) 'Perceived emotional intelligence, stress reactivity, and symptom reports: Further explorations using the Trait Meta-Mood Scale', *Psychology and Health,* 17 (5): 611–27.

Salzberger-Wittenberg, I., Henry, G. and Osborne, E. (1983) *The*

Emotional Experience of Learning and Teaching. London: Routledge & Kegan Paul.

Sartre, J.P. (1958) *Being and Nothingness.* Hazel E. Barnes (trans.). London: Methuen & Co. Ltd.

School Teachers Review Body (STRB) (2005) *Teachers Workload Diary Survey.* http://www.ome.uk.com/downloads/Teachers.9620workload 9620survey96202005.pdf. Accessed 3 September 2006.

Schore, A. (1994) *Affect Regulation and the Origin of the Self.* Hillsdale, NJ: Lawrence Erlbaum Associates Inc.

Schore, A. (1996) 'Experience dependent maturation of a regulatory mental psychopathology', *Development and Psychopathology,* 8: 59–87.

Scott Peck, M. (1985) *The Road Less Travelled.* Guernsey: Ryder and Co.

Seligman, M. (1975) *Helplessness: On depression, development and death.* San Francisco: Freeman.

Senge, P.M. (1990). *The Fifth Discipline: The art and practice of the learning organization.* New York: Doubleday.

Senge, P., Otto Scharmer, C. Jaworski, J. and Flowers, B.S. (2005) *Presence.* London: Nicholas Brealey Publishing.

Sennett, R. (1998) *The Corrosion of Character.* New York: Norton & Company.

Sergiovanni, T.J. (1992) *Moral Leadership: Getting to the heart of school reform.* San Francisco, CA: Jossey Bass.

Servan-Schreiber, D. (2004) *Healing without Freud or Prozac.* London: Rodale.

Shapiro, F. (1995) *Eye Movement Desensitization and Reprocessing (EMDR): Basic principles, protocols and procedures.* New York: Guilford Press.

Sharpe, K.E. and Schwartz, B. (2006) 'Practical Wisdom: Aristotle meets Positive Psychology', *Journal of Happiness Studies,* 7 (3): 377–39.

Siegel, D.J. and Hartzell, M. (2003) *Parenting from the Inside Out: How a deeper self-understanding can help you raise children who thrive.* New York: Penguin Putnam.

Simovska, V. and Sheehan, M. (2000) 'Worlds apart or of like minds? Health Promotion in Macedonian and Australian Schools', *Health Education,* 100 (5): 216–22.

Slaski, A.M. (2001) *An investigation into emotional intelligence, managerial stress and performance in a UK supermarket chain.* Unpublished PhD thesis, UMIST, Manchester.

Solms, M. (1996) 'Was sind die Affekte?' *Psyche,* 6 (50): 486–522.

Spalding, B. (2000) 'The contribution of a "Quiet Place" to early intervention strategies for children with emotional and behavioural difficulties in mainstream schools', *British Journal of Special Education*, 2 (3): 129–34.

Spillane, J. (2006) *Distributed Leadership*. San Francisco, CA: Jossey-Bass.

Stein, S. and Book, H. (2000) *The EQ Edge*. Toronto: Stoddart.

Stern, D. (1985) *The Interpersonal World of the Infant*. Basic Books: New York.

Sternberg, E. (2001). *The Balance Within*. New York: WH Freeman.

Stevens, J.O. (1971) *Awareness* Moab. Utah: Real People Press.

Strauss, A.L. and Corbin, J. (1990) *Basics of Qualitative Research: Grounded theory procedures and techniques*. Newbury Park: Sage Publications.

Sunderland, M. (2004) *Children's Mental Health*, Keynote Address: Counselling Children and Young People Annual Conference, London, November.

Teicher, M. (2000) www.researchmatters.harvard.edu

Teicher, M.H. (2000) 'Wounds that time won't heal: The neurobiology of child abuse', *Cerebrum*, 2 (4): 51–65.

Terrion, J.L. and Ashforth B.E. (2002) 'From 'I' to 'We': The role of putdown humour and identity in the development of a temporary group', *Human Relations*, 55 (1): 55–88.

Thomson, P., Harris, B. Vincent, K. and Toalster, R. (2005) *A Formative Evaluation of the Coalfields Alternatives to Exclusion (MATE) Strategy*. University of Nottingham: Centre for Research in Equity and Diversity Education.

Tomlinson, S. (2006) 'Another day, another White Paper', *Forum*, 48 (1): 49–54.

Tschannen-Moran, M. (2004) *Trust Matters*. San Fransisco, CA: Jossey-Bass.

TTA (1997) National Standards for Headteachers. London: HMSO.

Vedhara, K., Cox, N.K., Wilcock, G.K., Perks, P., Hunt, M., Anderson, S., Lightman, L. and Shanks, N.M. 'Chronic stress in elderly carers of dementia patients and antibody response to influenza vaccination', *Lancet*, Feb 20; 353 (9153): 627–31.

Watkins, C. (1999) 'Personal-social education: Beyond the National Curriculum', *British Journal of Guidance and Counselling*, 27 (1): 71–84.

Watkin, C. (2000) 'Developing emotional intelligence', *International Journal of Selection and Assessment*, 8 (2): 89–92.

Wenger, E., McDermott, R. and Snyder, W.M. (2002) *Cultivating*

Communities of Practice: A guide to managing knowledge. Boston, MA: Harvard Business School Press.

Wetz, J. (2006) *Holding Children in Mind Over Time.* Bristol: Bristol Education Initiative.

Wilkinson, G. (2005) 'Workforce remodelling and formal knowledge: the erosion of teachers' professional jurisdiction in English schools', *School Leadership and Management*, 25 (5): 421–40.

Williams, T. (2001) 'Unrecognized exodus, unaccepted accountability: The looming shortage of principals and vice principals in Ontario public school boards', Toronto: Ontario Principals Council.

Williamson, M. (1992) *A Return to Love.* New York: Harper Collin.

Winnicott, D.W. (1953) 'Transitional objects and transitional phenomena: A study of the first not-me possession', *International Journal of Psycho-Analysis*, 34: 89–97.

Winnicott, D.W. (1965) *The Maturational Process and the Facilitating Environment.* New York: International Universities Press.

Yontef, G. (1979) 'Gestalt Therapy: Clinical phenomenology', *The Gestalt Journal*, 21 (1): 27–45.

Yontef, G. (1993) *Awareness, Dialogue and Process.* Highland NY: The Gestalt Journal Press.

Young, M. and Wilmott, P. (1957) *Family and Kinship in East London.* London: Penguin.

Index